POLITICAL, RELIGIOUS,
AND CULTURAL BACKGROUND
HISTORY OF THE
NEW TESTAMENT BIBLE
(539 BC TO AD 135)

JONATHAN ORORODEKE

WESTBOW
P R E S S
A DIVISION OF THOMAS NELSON

Scripture taken from the King James Version of the Bible.

WestBow Press books may be ordered through booksellers or by contacting:

WestBow Press
A Division of Thomas Nelson
1663 Liberty Drive
Bloomington, IN 47403
www.westbowpress.com
1-(866) 928-1240

ISBN: 978-1-4908-0000-4 (sc)

Library of Congress Control Number: 2013911891

Printed in the United States of America.

WestBow Press rev. date: 7/1/13

ACKNOWLEDGEMENT

My greatest appreciation goes to the Almighty God who has graciously given me the wisdom, grace, knowledge and understanding in completing this book.

Also worthy of acknowledgement are: Pastor Awhinawhi Ari-Smart of Deeper Life Bible Church, Ughelli, Delta State of Nigeria (a Business Management Consultant), for his useful suggestions and corrections; and Rev. Edwin Edoja, General Overseer, Channel of Truth Ministries Inc., Ughelli, Delta State, Nigeria, for his careful editorial work of the whole script.

DEDICATION

I whole-heartedly dedicate this book to
my Creator, the Almighty God!

TABLE OF CONTENTS

Acknowledgement v

Dedication vi

Preface ix

Introduction.. xi

Chapter I: The Nature of New Testament Bible
Background History 1

    I.   Political Events 1

    II. Religious Events.................................... 2

    III. Cultural Events..................................... 4

Chapter II: Political Background History of the
New Testament Bible (539 BC to 135 AD).. 7

    I.   The Intertestamental Period (539
BC – 4 BC) 7

    II. The Gospel Period: 4 BC – AD
30 (Matthew - John)........................... 18

    III. The Church Period (AD 30 –
AD 100) 31

Chapter III: Religious Background History of the New Testament Bible (from 539 BC to 135 AD).. 39

    I.   The Intertestamental Period (539 BC – 4 BC) 39

    II. The Gospel Period: 4 BC – AD 30 (MATT 2:1-JN 21) 54

    III. The Church Period (AD 30 – AD 100) 69

Chapter IV: Cultural Background History of the New Testament Bible (from 539 BC to 135 AD).. 75

    I.   The Intertestamental Period (539 BC – 4 BC) 76

    II. The Gospel Period: 4 BC – AD 30 (MATT 2:1-JN 21) 77

    III. The Church Period (AD 30 – AD 100) 78

Chapter V: Recommendation....................................... 80

Bibliography.. 83

PREFACE

The Bible has become the most widely read Book in the world. This is as a result of its divine nature that has positively influenced human life on earth, leading to morally changed lives.

Despite its universal influence, it has remained the most **misunderstood**, **misinterpreted** and **misapplied** Book. This situation, no doubt, is caused by its dual nature of **Divine** (God) and **human** (man) in the writing process.

In order, therefore, to correct this issue of misinterpretation and misapplication of the Bible, after I had truly given my life to Christ in January, 1980, I took it upon myself as a major challenge to properly understand the main reason(s) people often misinterpret and misapply the Bible, which had caused several spiritual and moral problems in the lives of many believers of Christ down through the Christian period.

As a result of this, I became so interested in understanding the divine truths of the Bible, which got me busy with biblical studies even as a believer in the Church, until 5th February, 1993 when God eventually called me to full-time gospel ministry.

In the circumstance, I responded positively to the call, and then enrolled at a theological school in Benin City, Edo

State, Nigeria. While in school one afternoon in March, 1993, I had a vision and God divinely told me that He had given me the "Ministry of exposition of the Word of God", and that I should study the Bible at all times.

So after my graduation and subsequent posting to a branch church of my denomination; I took the Bible as the best of all books and actively involved myself in the teaching ministry of the Word of God.

Thus through the years of my studying and teaching of the Word of God, I have come to discover major interpretation issues associated with the Bible that must be cleared before the true biblical message can be properly understood and rightly applied for positive result.

It is this discovery that then led me to do further theological research to properly confirm my discovery, and of course, I got the confirmation from various theological sources that really gave me the full confidence in writing this book.

Firstly, the purpose of this book is to put the New Testament Bible in its proper *political*, *religious* and *cultural* settings to enable certificate, diploma and degree students of theology as well as ministers of the gospel, Sunday School Teachers, Bible Study Teachers and indeed all Bible-loving people generally, have right understanding in interpreting the New Testament Scriptures which will produce more positive and lasting spiritual results in the lives of believers of Christ.

Secondly, it is also to close up the *political*, *religious* and *cultural* gaps for readers and students of the New Testament Bible, and easily identify and understand **names of people, places** and **events** concerning the New Testament political, religious and cultural background!

Introduction

"Political, Religious and Cultural Background History of the New Testament Bible" is a book on the First Century biblical history from the Intertestamental period (end of Malachi) to the New Testament Bible Book of Revelation.

The book which has four chapters focuses on the political, religious and cultural events of the New Testament Bible, which are major problems in biblical interpretation.

Chapter One: **"The Nature of New Testament Bible Background History"**. This chapter explains what New Testament Bible background history is really about. It is the study of first century historical events which took place in the New Testament Bible period from the end of the Old Testament Bible Book of Malachi to the New Testament Bible Book of Revelation.

In this chapter, the political, religious and cultural background or setting of the New Testament Bible from Matthew to Revelation is clearly outlined, to assist Bible lovers to be well guided in their proper study and interpretation of the New Testament Bible.

Chapter Two: **Political Background History of the New Testament Bible.** This chapter takes a careful look at the different world empires (from Persian Empire to the

Roman Empire), which had ruled the nation of Israel at different periods of her political history.

Also considered are the positive and negative political influences that these empires had on the general lives of Israel.

Chapter Three: **Religious Background History of the New Testament Bible.** Here, consideration is given to the positive and negative religious effects that these empires had on the religious life of the nation of Israel.

Chapter Four: **Cultural Background History of the New Testament Bible.** In this chapter, a study of the positive and negative cultural effects that the empires had on the religious life of the nation of Israel, are carefully examined.

Chapter Five: **Recommendation.** This chapter is only a recommendation to my audience of the series on "understanding the New Testament Bible" I intend to work on.

Therefore, the present book "Political, Religious and Cultural Background History of the New Testament Bible" is the first in this series. And it is recommended that interested persons can get copies as soon as they are made available.

CHAPTER I

THE NATURE OF NEW TESTAMENT BIBLE BACKGROUND HISTORY

New Testament Bible background history deals with the study of historical events that took place in New Testament Bible times from the Persian Empire's reign over the affairs of Israel during the Intertestament Period to Bar Kochba's Revolt, which covered the period of approximately 539 BC to AD 135. But note, the New Testament Bible Period proper, closed at AD 100; which is the **First Century** biblical history under review.

These historical events, therefore, are covered in three different sections – political, religious and cultural events respectively.

I.   POLITICAL EVENTS

Through military attack or battle, three world empires took over the political administration of the nation of Israel from the Intertestamental period to the end of the New Testament Book of Revelation. And these world powers were the Persian, Greek and Roman Empires.

Thus, the Persian Empire took over from the Babylonian Empire, while the Greek Empire took over from the Persian Empire. In the same manner, the Roman Empire took over from the Greek Empire. This was the order of the military journey of the three Empires.

Out of these empires, the Roman Empire had the greatest influence on the political life of the people of Israel, because Rome had already taken over Israel's leadership before even Christ was born. And it continued in leadership till AD 100, and beyond.

Clearly, this means that from the Ministry of Christ in the Gospels to the end of the New Testament Book of Revelation (AD 100), it was **only** the Roman Empire that was fully in-charge of the political affairs of Israel (Palestine).

Below is an outline of the New Testament political setting covering 539 BC to AD 100, for clearer understanding:

A. INTERTESTAMENTAL PERIOD (BETWEEN MALACHI AND MATTHEW): 539 BC - 4 BC

1. Persian Rule
2. Greek Rule
3. Roman Rule

B. GOSPEL PERIOD (MATTHEW – JOHN): 4 BC – AD 30

1. Roman Rule

C. CHURCH PERIOD (ACTS – REVELATION): AD 30 – AD 100

1. Roman Rule

II. RELIGIOUS EVENTS

The New Testament religious events are influenced by three religions, which are the Jewish, Greek and Roman religions.

As we know, Jewish religion is another name for Judaism, which simply means the religion of the Jews or people of Israel. This was the main religion of the Jews.

Fortunately, when the Persian Empire took over Israel, the Jews were given freedom of worship by the Empire. Also during the days of the Greek Empire under Alexander the Great, this same freedom was extended to them. Even after the death of Alexander the Great, when his kingdom was divided among his four army generals (Lysimachus, Cassander, Ptolemy and Seleucus); the Jews under the leadership of the Ptolemaic Empire, headed by Ptolemy were allowed to continue with their religion.

Unfortunately, when the Seleucid Empire, headed by Seleucus took over the whole territory, the Jews now paid dearly for their past religious freedom, when the empire seized all religious rights from them, and then demanded that they **must** worship the Greek god "Zeus". This created a terrible religious situation for the Jews.

Eventually, when the Roman Empire, through General Pompe took over the leadership of Israel, the Jews were never religiously maltreated like the Seleucid Empire, but allowed them to have their freedom of worship, while the Roman Empire themselves practiced what is known as **Greco-Roman religion**, which is a combination of both Greek and Roman religious practices.

Thus, the New Testament Bible, from the time of Christ to the end of the Book of Revelation, the three religions that influenced its background, are the Jewish Religion (Judaism), Christian Religion (Christianity) and Greco-Roman Religion.

Find below an outline showing the New Testament religious setting from 539 BC to AD 100:

A. **INTERTESTAMENTAL PERIOD (BETWEEN MALACHI AND MATTHEW): 539 BC - 4 BC**

1. Jewish Religion (Judaism)
2. Greek Religion
3. Greco-Roman Religion

B. **GOSPEL PERIOD (MATTHEW – JOHN): 4 BC – AD 30**

1. Jewish Religion

C. **CHURCH PERIOD (ACTS – REVELATION): AD 30 – AD 100**

1. Jewish Religion (Judaism)
2. Christian Religion (Christianity)
3. Greco-Roman Religion

III. CULTURAL EVENTS

The New Testament cultural events are influenced by three cultures, which are the Jewish, Greek and Roman cultures.

In the Intertestamental Period, when Alexander the Great was in-charge of the Greek Empire, both Jewish and Greek cultural practices were fully recognized.

When the Roman Empire took over leadership of Israel, because they had fallen in love with the Greek culture, they were forced to allow both the Jewish and Greek cultural practices to continue.

In addition, the Roman authority decided to adopt an improved culture for the Empire which included a combination of both Greek and Roman cultural practices, resulting in the formation of a Greco-Roman cultural system.

Therefore, the New Testament, from Matthew to the Book of Revelation, has only two major cultures that influenced its background: the Jewish and Greco-Roman cultures.

Find below an outline showing the New Testament cultural setting:

A. INTERTESTAMENTAL PERIOD (BETWEEN MALACHI AND MATTHEW): 539 BC - 4 BC

1. Jewish Culture
2. Greek Culture
3. Greco-Roman Culture

B. GOSPEL PERIOD (MATTHEW – JOHN): 4 BC – AD 30

1. Jewish Culture
2. Greco-Roman Culture

C. CHURCH PERIOD (ACTS – REVELATION): AD 30 – AD 100

1. Jewish Culture
2. Greco-Roman Culture

As we properly understand the New Testament Bible in its political, religious and cultural settings, only then are we able to interpret and apply it correctly.

Sincerely speaking, understanding and applying the Bible correctly is a serious matter that we must never pay lip-service to. The problem on our hands right now, is for us to know how to reconcile the New Testament Bible historical events of the ancient **First Century** world with our civilized **21st Century** world. In fact, in order for us to understand the New Testament Scriptures properly, we must first understand the historical events of the **1st Century** world in which the New Testament Bible was written. This will then guide us in interpreting and applying the Scriptures correctly, which will bring definite spiritual transformation in our personal lives as well as others.

CHAPTER II

POLITICAL BACKGROUND HISTORY OF THE NEW TESTAMENT BIBLE (539 BC TO 135 AD)

I. THE INTERTESTAMENTAL PERIOD (539 BC – 4 BC)

For us to properly understand the intertestamental history, we shall first have an idea of the term "**Intertestamental Period**." This is the term used for the 400-year period between the prophecy of prophet Malachi concerning the coming of Elijah in the Old Testament book of Malachi 4:5 and the announcement of the birth of **John the Baptist** by angel Gabriel in the New Testament book of Lk 1:11-20, which covers the period of about 539 BC "(5th Century BC)" to 4 BC "(1st Century AD)". *(Note: "BC" means "Before Christ," and "AD" means "Anno Domini" in Greek language, which is interpreted as "the year of our Lord".*

The political history, therefore, as it concerns the New Testament Bible background during the 400 years Intertestamental period will be given in summary. The reason is that the writer wishes to give only the key points and not the overall historical details, just to open up the scriptural background of the New Testament Bible to enable theological college students, ministers of the gospel, as well as all Christians, have proper and balanced understanding in interpreting and applying the New Testament Scriptures.

Indeed, the Intertestamental Period was actually a very trying period for the people of Israel politically. During this period, the nation experienced a lot of foreign pagan military rules.

The political chronology or line of events of this period therefore, took the following order - **Persian rule**, **Greek rule**, **Jewish Independence**, and **Roman rule**:

A. POLITICAL TRANSITION HISTORY FROM PERSIAN TO ROMAN RULE IN ISRAEL

After the Babylonian captivity of the people of Israel which lasted from 626 BC to 539 BC (**87** years), the nation of Israel experienced the rules of successive foreign military world powers in her political life.

These powers included the **Persian Empire** (539 BC – 359 BC (**180** years), **Greek Empire** (359 BC – 166 BC (**293** years), *a break period called* **Jewish Independence or Self-government** (166 BC – 63 BC (**103** years), and the **Roman Empire** (63 BC – AD 100 (**37** years and beyond).

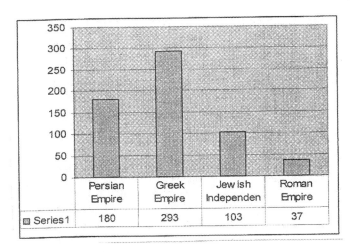

	Persian Empire	Greek Empire	Jewish Independen	Roman Empire
☐ Series1	180	293	103	37

Years of rule of the Empires in the Intertestamental Period

It is very sad to say that each of all these world powers took over the political leadership of the nation of Israel through military attack or battle:

1. **Persian rulership over Israel (539 BC – 359 BC)**

The Babylonian empire was the world power in control of the nation's political affairs from 626 BC to 539 BC when the Israelites went into captivity in Babylon. But at the time the remnants (Ezra the priest and leader, Nehemiah and Zerubbabel), returned from Babylon to the land of Israel (*Palestine*), another world power (*the Persian Empire*) was already in-charge. The Persian Empire ruled from 539 BC to 359 BC, when eventually the Greek Empire, through military power and might, took over the mantle of leadership; thus, bringing to an end the Persian Empire's political reign.

2. **Greek Rulership over Israel (359 BC –166 BC)**

   a. **King Philip II of Macedon (359 BC – 336 BC)**

   The Greek Empire was established as one inseparable political empire by the personal efforts of "Philip of Macedon" in the country of ancient Macedonia which is now known as Greece in our world. He ruled the empire from 359 BC to 336 BC, a period of about **23** years.

   Unfortunately, he was brutally killed in a very bloody military war that took place in 336 BC between the Persian and Greek Empires.

   b. **Alexander the Great (336 BC – 323 BC)**

   Alexander the Great took over the leadership of the Greek Empire after the death of his father, King Philip II in 336 BC.

   Alexander, who was a very great military leader, displayed his military ability in fighting so many wars and captured various lands to expand his political territory.

   During his reign, Alexander the Great influenced his people (subjects), among who were the people of Israel, with the *Greek culture*. In other words, the major focus of his political administration over his people was "Hellenization" or "Hellenism", which is "*Greek civilization and culture* embracing *dress, theaters, gymnasium, stadiums, language and religion*". Really, this policy of "*Hellenization*" provided an open door, by means of the Greek language, for the spread of Christianity in the New Testament period!

But, he ruled for about **13** years and died in 323 BC.

c. Division of Alexander's Empire

After the death of Alexander the Great, there was a serious power struggle among his four army generals: **Ptolemy**, **Lysimachus**, **Cassander**, and **Seleucus**, about who should succeed him. It was very sad for Alexander the Great to have lost his **only** son before his death, who should have been the right person to continue his political dynasty after his death. Thus, this unexpected incident created a very big political problem in the Empire.

However, the Greek Empire was divided among his four generals according to the vision of Daniel (Dan 8:8):

*"Therefore the he goat waxed very great: and when he was strong, the great horn was broken; and for it came up **four** notable ones toward the four winds of heaven."*

(1) **Lysimachus** was given Thrace and Asia Minor.
(2) **Cassander** received Macedonia.
Note: Not much can be known about the history of these two rulers (Lysimachus and Cassander) in the kingdom.

(3) **Ptolemy** got Egypt, Cyrenaica, Palestine, Phoenicia, Cyprus and some parts of western Asia Minor including the Aegean Sea of Palestine. He ruled in the Ptolemaic Kingdom from 324 BC to 264 BC (**60** years).

(4) **Seleucus** was given Babylonia and Syria to the north including east of Palestine. He ruled in the Seleucid Kingdom from 204 BC to 166 BC (**38** years). During this period, Israel (*Palestine*) went through a time of **great sufferings** – politically, religiously, physically and otherwise.

3. Maccabean Revolt and Rule (Jewish Independence): 166 BC – AD 63

Following the continuous sufferings of the people of Israel in the hands of the Seleucid authority, Mattathias, a priest from the priestly family of Hasmonean in Jerusalem along with his five sons (John, Simon, Judas, Eleazer and Jonathan), also supported by some other Jews who stood against Greek cultural practices (Hellenism), started a **revolt** against the Seleucid authority to stop the continuous maltreatment and sufferings of the Israelites. They were very successful in the operation, but only after a heavy fighting. (**Note:** This kind of **revolt** could be interpreted as "insurrection," which is rising against a constituted authority. In other words, it is *"a rebellion*, a *revolution, a mutiny, an uprising", or* *even a "civil disobedience"* against a legal authority that would undoubtedly attract the punishment of death).

Nevertheless, this bold act of Mattathias, his five sons and the Jewish supporters, made way for the **Jewish Independence** and subsequently the Maccabean rule in Palestine from 166 BC to 63 BC (a period of **103** years).

Unfortunately, **General Pompey** of the Roman army, following a civil war that broke out within the Maccabean kingdom, decided to seize the opportunity to carry out a deadly military attack on the Jewish Independent kingdom and then successfully took over Palestine in 63 BC.

4. Roman rulership over Israel (63 BC – 4 BC)

After Rome had succeeded in taking over the land of Palestine, she became the major world power from 63 BC to 4 BC (approximately **59** years). During this period, Rome appointed **Hyrcanus II** who was a member of the Hasmonean priestly family, as high priest and political ruler of the Jews; while **Antipater** *(a member of the family line of Esau, an Edomite)* was appointed Governor of Judea. At the same time, Antipater's two sons: **Phasael** and **Herod**, were also appointed into positions of leadership - Phasael was appointed Governor of Jerusalem while Herod was appointed Governor of Galilee.

Immediately after these appointments were made, there was a sudden military attack on Jerusalem by the Hasmonean political leadership, and Jerusalem was accordingly conquered by them. In the process, Hyrcanus II and Phasael were killed, but Herod managed to escape to Rome for safety. While there, he made his political intentions known to Emperors Antony and Octavian, and was accordingly appointed king of Judea by the Roman Senate, along with a military back-up.

With all the joy in his heart of being a king over Israel, he came back from Rome to Judea to begin his rule. But to his greatest surprise, he met his opponents, the Hasmonean leadership, already in- charge of the nation's affairs. As a result of this development, there was no way for him to settle down to rule until 37 BC, when fortunately through the backing up of a group of Roman soldiers, he was able to take over and began his political career till 4 BC.

As a matter of fact, King Herod the Great was from the family line of Esau. That is, he was an Edomite and not an Israelite or Israeli.

During his kingly reign over Israel, he did so many good things for the people of Israel, at least, to buy their mind over in favour of his throne, as well as impressing on the Roman authority of his political achievements. Among these were: *"rebuilding of Samaria, which he also named Sebast; construction of an artificial harbour for Caesarea; building of fortresses; reconstruction of a high standard Temple in Jerusalem"*. Herod started the reconstruction of this temple in 20 BC till 4 BC (approximately **16** years). After his death, the project continued until AD 64, when it was completed. On the whole, the project lasted for approximately 46 years, as recorded in Jn 2:20 *"Then said the Jews, **Forty and six years** was this temple in building, and wilt thou rear it up in three days?"*

On the contrary side, the Jews did not like him so much, just because of his non-Jewish lineage, coupled with the fact that he was never interested in favouring Judaism, their religion. Rather, he favoured "**Hellenism**," which is the promotion of the *"Greek culture, philosophy, language, and history"*.

Naturally speaking, Herod was a man that was **very jealous** of his kingly throne. To this end, he was **always suspicious** of people supposedly trying to overthrow him on the throne. **In addition, he was an ambitious** man or a man of **high taste, mercilessly wicked** or **brutal** and **highly trickish.** As a result of all these serious moral faults in him, he had always fought very hard to *secure* his throne at all cost: *he had never taken it lightly with anyone who was ever discovered or suspected of being used to carry out any kind of political coup against his throne, that would lead to his dethronement.*

Above all, having no fear of God, as well as no regard for human life, he killed **two** of his ten wives, **three** of his fifteen sons, his father-in-law, his mother-in-law, and his brother-in-law. He also killed many of his close friends, his rivals *(those who were likely to compete for his throne)*, revolutionaries, and all those who had ever criticized his bad leadership style. In addition, he killed 45 Rabbis (Jewish Teachers) who were members of the **Sanhedrin**.

(The Sanhedrin is a Jewish Supreme Court with a membership of 70 persons made up of the Pharisees, Sadducees and Scribes, excluding the high priest who is head of the Council).

In fact, it was because of this **jealous**, **suspicious**, **wicked** and **no rival** attitude in him, which led him to kill the innocent male children of two (2) years and below in Bethlehem of Judea, during the birth of Christ in Matt. 2:1-18.

He was said to have ruled for **34** years, and finally died in 4 BC at the age of **69** years "*(73 BC to 4 BC)*", as a result of a very serious disease. Although there was no accurate medical explanation of the type of his disease, but medical experts had proposed different medical terms to describe the disease like: *"chronic kidney disease, chronic cancer; syphilis, ulceration of the intestines, gastro-intestinal disease, and dropsy".*

In effect, the end of King Herod the Great's reign in 4 BC can be said that the New Testament Bible's political, religious and cultural background history truly started from this point!

SPECIAL NOTE

The Roman government was not like the Greek government that enforced its culture on the Jews, but allowed them to practice their own culture and religion. The only requirements that the authority demanded from the Jews included payment of tax and obedience to Roman laws.

As a result of this, King Herod the Great, in order to generate enough money for his expensive construction works, introduced high tax rate for the Jews.

Thus, the authority to collect tax from the Jews was then given or contracted to the Sadducees by King Herod. The Sadducees in turn hired tax collectors (**publicans**) for the job. Herod's government had a particular fixed tax rate. So after all the tax was collected, Herod's government would take her share, and then the Sadducees theirs too. In turn, out of their own share, the Sadducees would give the tax collectors their share.

But to make more money for themselves, the dubious or corrupt tax collectors deliberately increased the tax rate higher than the officially approved rate (Lk 3:12-13):

> *"Then came also **publicans** to be baptized, and said unto him, Master, what shall we do? And he said unto them, **Exact no more than that which is appointed you**."*

The effect of this criminal act of the tax collectors greatly reduced the economic life of the Jews, as a **very high tax rate** was now paid by them; while both the Sadducees and tax collectors made enough money to live comfortably!

This poor economic situation in Israel made the Jews to develop serious hatred for the tax collectors until the time of Christ in the Gospels, as recorded in Matt. 9:9-11:

*"And as Jesus passed forth from thence, he saw a man, named Matthew, sitting at the receipt of **custom**: and he saith unto him, Follow me. And he arose, and followed him. And it came to pass, as Jesus sat at meat in the house, behold, many **publicans** and sinners came and sat down with him and his disciples. And when the **Pharisees** saw it, they said unto his disciples, Why eateth your Master with **publicans** and sinners?"*

II. THE GOSPEL PERIOD: 4 BC – AD 30 (MATTHEW - JOHN)

As at the time of the birth and ministry of Jesus, the Roman Empire was the **only** political world-power controlling the affairs of the nation of Israel.

Geographically, the Jews occupied the territory of Judea in the Roman Empire which was a sub-province to Syria as at that time. But during the reign of King Herod Agrippa I in the Book of Acts of the Apostles, Judea became a separate or an autonomous province.

Politically, the autonomous province of Judea experienced three major wars between the Jews and the Roman authority. These were the "**First Jewish Revolt**" of AD 66 – AD 70 (**4** years); the "**Kitos War**" of AD 115 – AD 117 (**2** years); and the "**Second Jewish Revolt**" also known as the "**Bar Kochba's Revolt**" of AD 132 – AD 135 (**3** years).

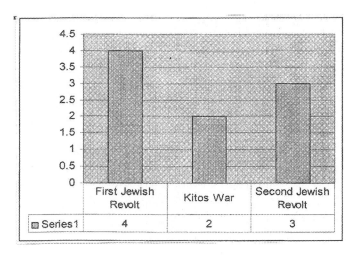

	First Jewish Revolt	Kitos War	Second Jewish Revolt
Series1	4	2	3

Years of the three Wars

Historically, from the end of the Intertestamental Period, and stretching further into the Church Period (Matthew - Acts 26), the political dynasty in place at this time, was the Herodian dynasty, that is, *rule of the Herods* involving Herod the Great, Herod Archelaus, Herod Antipas, Herod Philip, Herod Agrippa I (grand-son) and Herod Agrippa II (great grand-son). From all indications, the Herodian dynasty ended with the death of Herod Agrippa II in AD 92 (Acts 26):

A. DIVISION OF HEROD THE GREAT'S KINGDOM

After the death of Herod the Great, the kingdom was divided among **only** three of his chosen sons (Archelaus, Antipas and Philip), out of his fifteen sons:

1. **Herod Archelaus** received three regions - Samaria, Judea and Idumea as "ethnarch" (*ruler of the people*):

   a. **Samaria Region**
      (1) Meggido
      (2) Dothan
      (3) Salim
      (4) Sychar
      (5) Antipatris (Aphek)
      (6) Alexandrium

   b. **Judea Region**
      (1) Lydda
      (2) Bethel
      (3) Ephraim
      (4) Berea
      (5) Jericho
      (6) Emmaus
      (7) Cyprus
      (8) Jerusalem
      (9) Bethany
      (10) Bethlehem
      (11) Hyrcannia
      (12) Herodium
      (13) Hebron
      (14) Engedi
      (15) Joppa

c. Idumea Region

    (1) Masada

    (2) Arad

    (3) Beersheba

    (4) Malatha

2. Herod Antipas was given two regions - Galilee and Perea as "tetrarch" (*ruler in-charge of four provinces):*

a. Galilee Region

    (1) Hazor

    (2) Chorazin

    (3) Gennesaret

    (4) Capernaum

    (5) Magdala

    (6) Cana

    (7) Tiberias

    (8) Nazareth

    (9) Nain

b. Perea Region

    (1) Amataus

    (2) Bethabara

    (3) Esbus(Heshbon)

    (4) Machaerus

3. **Herod Philip** got three gentile regions to the east of the Sea of Galilee - Iturea, Gaulanitis and Trachonitis also as "tetrarch":

    a. **Iturea Region**

        (1) Ceesarea

    b. **Gaulantis Region**

        (1) Bethsaida
        (2) Gergasa

    c. **Trachonitis Region**

        (1) Raphana

Here is a brief history on the extent of political reigns of the three sons within their individual territory:

1. **Herod Archelaus**

Herod Archelaus ruled from 4 BC to AD 6 (a period of **10** years). It was this Herod who was ruling over the region of Judea when God told Joseph to take Child Jesus back from Egypt to the land of Israel, but because he was afraid of his wicked character, ***just like his father, Herod the Great was***, Joseph had to go and stay in Nazareth of the region of Galilee under Herod Antipas, after having been warned by God in a dream not to go into the region of Judea under Herod Archelaus (Matt. 2:19-23):

> *"But when Herod was **dead**, behold, an angel of the Lord appeareth in a dream to Joseph in Egypt, Saying, Arise, and take the young child and his*

*mother, and go into the **land of Israel**: for they are **dead** which sought the **young child's life**. And he arose, and took the young child and his mother, and came into the land of Israel. But when he heard that **Archelaus** did reign in Judaea in the room of his father Herod, he was afraid to go thither: notwithstanding, being warned of God in a dream, he turned aside into the parts of Galilee: And he came and dwelt in a city called Nazareth: that it might be fulfilled which was spoken by the prophets, He shall be called a Nazarene".*

In AD 6, Archelaus was removed from office and banished to "Vienne in Gaul (France)" by the Roman military government, because he was found to be very wicked to the Jews; and then series of Roman governors or procurators were appointed to oversee his territory.

Pontius Pilate was said to be the fifth of such governors to rule this territory from AD 26 – AD 36 (**10** years):

> **Matt 27:1-2** *"When the morning was come, all the chief priests and elders of the people took counsel against Jesus to put him to death: And when they had bound him, they led him away, and delivered him to **Pontius Pilate** the governor;"*

During Pilate's reign, he killed so many people who were against his wicked practices, being a very wicked leader. Among such innocent people were the **Galileans**, that he mercilessly killed in the temple as they were offering their sacrifices in worship of Jehovah (Luke 13:1-3):

> *"There were present at that season some that told him of the* **Galilaeans**, *whose blood* **Pilate** *had mingled with their sacrifices. And Jesus answering said unto them, Suppose ye that these Galilaeans were sinners above all the Galilaeans, because they suffered such things? I tell you, Nay: but, except ye repent, ye shall all likewise perish".*

2. Herod Antipas

Herod Antipas ruled from 4 BC – AD 39 (a period of **43** years). Scriptural passages that bear record of his political activities are: Matt. 14:1-12; Mk 6:14-29; Lk 3:1, 19; 9:7-9; 13:32; 23:6-12; Acts 13:1.

It was this Herod who reluctantly killed John the Baptist, being accused of illegally marrying his brother, Philip's wife (this Philip was a half-brother of Herod Antipas), as clearly recorded in Mk 6:17-29:

> *"For* **Herod** *himself had sent forth and laid hold upon John, and bound him in prison for Herodias' sake, his brother Philip's wife: for he had married her. For John had said unto* **Herod**, *It is not lawful for thee to have thy brother's wife. Therefore Herodias had a quarrel against him, and would have killed him; but she could not: For* **Herod** *feared John, knowing that he was a just man and an holy, and observed him; and when he heard him, he did many things, and heard him gladly.*

*And when a convenient day was come, that **Herod** on his birthday made a supper to his lords, high captains, and chief estates of Galilee; And when the daughter of the said Herodias came in, and danced, and pleased **Herod** and them that sat with him, the king said unto the damsel, Ask of me whatsoever thou wilt, and I will give it thee. And he sware unto her, Whatsoever thou shalt ask of me, I will give it thee, unto the half of my kingdom. And she went forth, and said unto her mother, What shall I ask? And she said, The head of John the Baptist. And she came in straightway with haste unto the king, and asked, saying, I will that thou give me by and by in a charger the head of John the Baptist. And the king was exceeding sorry; yet for his oath's sake, and for their sakes which sat with him, he would not reject her. And immediately the king sent an executioner, and commanded his head to be brought: and he went and beheaded him in the prison, And brought his head in a charger, and gave it to the damsel: and the damsel gave it to her mother. And when his disciples heard of it, they came and took up his corpse, and laid it in a tomb".*

Jesus addressed him as a "**fox**" in Luke 13:32:

*"And he said unto them, Go ye, and tell that **fox**, Behold, I cast out devils, and I do cures to day and to morrow, and the third day I shall be perfected".*

Herod Antipas was the one who presided over the trial of Jesus in Lk 23:7-12. He was removed from office by the Roman authority and "banished to Lyons, Gaul" in AD 39.

3. Herod Philip

Herod Philip ruled from 4 BC – AD 34 (**38** years): Lk 3:1 *"Now in the fifteenth year of the reign of Tiberius Caesar, Pontius Pilate being governor of Judaea, and Herod being tetrarch of Galilee, and his brother **Philip** tetrarch of Ituraea and of the region of Trachonitis, and Lysanias the tetrarch of Abilene,".* He died in AD 34.

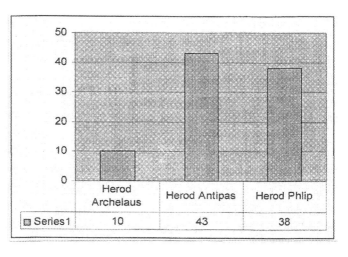

Years of rule of Herod the Great's three sons

4. Herodians

Herodians were a group of Jews who joined hands together with the Sadducees to form a united force, and submitted themselves to the authority of the Roman government, as well as being loyal supporters of the leadership of the Herods to remain on the throne.

Sometimes, the Pharisees usually used this same group to their advantage, by sending them to trap Jesus in His speaking, in order to have opportunity of accusing Him of speaking against the Roman authority, and then deal with Him accordingly. At other times, they would join themselves with the Herodians to plan Jesus' death. The evidence is clear from Scripture:

> **Matt. 22:16** *"And they sent out unto him their disciples with the **Herodians**, saying, Master, we know that thou art true, and teachest the way of God in truth, neither carest thou for any man: for thou regardest not the person of men."*

> **Mk 3:6** *"And the Pharisees went forth, and straightway took counsel with the **Herodians** against him, how they might destroy him."*

> **Mk 12:13** *"And they send unto him certain of the Pharisees and of the **Herodians**, to catch him in his words."*

B. APPOINTMENT OF EMPERORS BY THE ROMAN SENATE

Several Emperors were appointed by the Roman Senate to oversee the affairs of the whole Empire at different periods of Roman political history.

Once appointed, an Emperor automatically possesses superior powers over Rome, including being a commander-in-chief of the entire Roman legions or armed forces. Other titles used in addressing the Emperor included *"Augustus, Caesar, and Princeps"*.

Both from biblical and external evidences, eight (8) Emperors were appointed to rule the Roman Empire during the New Testament Bible period (*Matthew to Revelation*); and they either positively or negatively affected Jewish political, religious and cultural history.

Two of these Emperors *(Augustus and Tiberius)*, ruled during the time of the **Gospels** (Matthew to John), while the remaining six *(Caligula, Claudius, Nero, Vespasian, Titus and Domitian)* ruled during the **Church Age** (Acts to Revelation). Although the names of **Caligula**, **Nero**, **Vespasian**, **Titus** and **Domitian** might not appear in the New Testament Bible, yet they were well involved in the administration of the Empire.

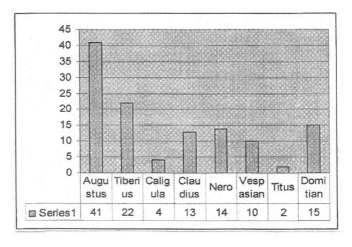

	Augustus	Tiberius	Caligula	Claudius	Nero	Vespasian	Titus	Domitian
Series1	41	22	4	13	14	10	2	15

Years of rule of the Ceasars

1. Augustus Caesar (27 BC – AD 14)

Augustus Caesar was appointed by the Roman government to rule over Rome including Palestine Israel, from 27 BC to AD 14, a period of **41** years, see Acts 25:8, 11, 21, 25; 27:1. An army of 28 legions *(a legion is an army division that is made up of 3 or 6,000 soldiers)* was said to have been directly placed under his command at that time. And during his reign, the whole empire experienced great peace and prosperity.

However he was responsible for some historical events which took place in Israel:

a. He ordered for a national census which eventually led to Jesus being born in Bethlehem of Judea (Lk 2:1-7):

*"And it came to pass in those days, that there went out a decree from **Caesar Augustus**, that all the world should be taxed. (And this taxing was first made when Cyrenius was governor of Syria.) And all went to be taxed, every one into his own city. And Joseph also went up from Galilee, out of the city of Nazareth, into Judaea, unto the city of David, which is called Bethlehem; (because he was of the house and lineage of David:) To be taxed with Mary his espoused wife, being great with child. And so it was, that, while they were there, the days were accomplished that she should be delivered. And she brought forth her firstborn son, and wrapped him in swaddling clothes, and laid*

him in a manger; because there was no room for them in the inn".

b. He introduced a special monetary system of coins that carried his image and inscription (Matt. 22:17-21):

> *"Tell us therefore, What thinkest thou? Is it lawful to give tribute unto Caesar, or not? But Jesus perceived their wickedness, and said, Why tempt ye me, ye hypocrites? Shew me the tribute money. And they brought unto him a penny. And he saith unto them, Whose is this **image** and **superscription**? They say unto him, **Caesar's**. Then saith he unto them, Render therefore unto Caesar the things which are Caesar's; and unto God the things that are God's".*

2. Tiberius Caesar (AD 14 – AD 37): Lk 3:1

Tiberius Caesar ruled for 22 years, from AD 14 to AD 37. During his reign, all the peace and prosperity that the Empire had once enjoyed in the time of Augustus Caesar, suddenly disappeared and a time of bitter experience was mysteriously introduced by him. This was possible because of his wicked leadership style.

It was in the time of Tiberius Caesar that John the Baptist started his preaching ministry (Lk 3:1-2):

> *"Now in the fifteenth year of the reign of **Tiberius Caesar**, Pontius Pilate being governor of Judaea, and Herod being tetrarch of Galilee, and his*

brother Philip tetrarch of Ituraea and of the region
of Trachonitis, and Lysanias the tetrarch of Abilene,
Annas and Caiaphas being the high priests, the
word of God came unto John the son of Zacharias
in the wilderness".

Also the ministry, death, burial, crucifixion,
resurrection and subsequent ascension of Christ took
place during Emperor Tiberius' rule.

III. THE CHURCH PERIOD (AD 30 – AD 100)

A. KING HEROD AGRIPPA I (AD 37 - AD 44): ACTS 2:1-24

The continuation of Herod the Great's political
dynasty is seen through Herod Agrippa I, the grand-
son of Herod the Great and Mariamne, and a nephew
to both Herod Philip and Herod Antipas. His father was
Aristobolus, the son of Herod the Great. Drusilla was
a daughter to Agrippa I who was married to Felix, the
Roman Governor according to Acts 24:24.

Herod Agrippa I was appointed King over Palestine
(Iturea, Gaulanitis, Trachonitis, Galilee, and Perea), the
territory of his late uncle, *Herod Philip,* by the Roman
military government from AD 37 to AD 44, a period of
7 years (Acts 12:1-6, 18-24; 12:21-23).

It was this Herod who succeeded in killing Apostle
James, the brother of John, whose father was Zebedee.
Not satisfied, he went further to capture and imprisoned
Apostle Peter. This led the church to go into serious time
of prayer for Peter's immediate deliverance from the

powers of physical death in the hands of Herod Agrippa I (Acts 12:1-5):

> "Now about that time **Herod** the king stretched forth his hands to vex certain of the church. And he killed James the brother of John with the sword. And because he saw it pleased the Jews, he proceeded further to take Peter also. (Then were the days of unleavened bread.) And when he had apprehended him, he put him in prison, and delivered him to four quaternions of soldiers to keep him; intending after Easter to bring him forth to the people. Peter therefore was kept in prison: but prayer was made without ceasing of the church unto God for him".

Because of pride, King Herod Agrippa I took the praise and glory that belonged to God alone. Being angry, God sent an angel to afflict him with a terrible disease which eventually led to his death in AD 44 (Acts 12:21-23):

> "And upon a set day **Herod**, arrayed in royal apparel, sat upon his throne, and made an oration unto them. And the people gave a shout, saying, It is the voice of a god, and not of a man. And immediately the angel of the Lord smote him, because he gave not God the glory: and he was eaten of worms, and gave up the ghost".

B. APPOINTMENT OF ROMAN GOVERNORS (AD 52 – AD 62)

After the death of King Herod Agrippa I, his political territory was added to the province of Syria, and two Roman governors (*Antonius Felix and Porcius Festus*), were appointed to rule the territory under the supervision of the Proconsul (Provincial Head) of Syria:

1. **Felix (AD 52 – AD 60): Acts 23:24-26, 34; 24:2-3, 22, 24-27; 25:14**

Governor Antonius Felix ruled for **8** years, from AD 52 – AD 60, during which he presided over Paul's trial. He also heard the Apostle's gospel message and trembled at the word of God, but never accepted it (Acts chapters 24-25).

2. **Festus (AD 60 – AD 62): Acts 24:24-25:12**

Governor Porcius Festus ruled for only **2** years, from AD 60 to AD 62. He was the second governor to hear Paul's case (Acts 25). He recommended that Paul should be taken back to Jerusalem for trial. However, he did this in order to make the Jews happy.

Furthermore, all the governors were regarded as bad administrators, because they did not rule their individual territories according to the wish of the Roman government that appointed them, rather they ruled to satisfy their own selfish interests.

For history sake, below is a list of other Roman Governors and their respective tenure of office, who served in the political administration of the Empire:

1. Coponius (AD 6 – AD 10)
2. M. Ambivius (AD 10 – AD 13)
3. Annius Rufus (AD 13 – AD 15)
4. Valerius Gratus (AD 15 – AD 26)

5.   Marcellus (AD 36 – AD 38)
6.   Maryllus (AD 38 – AD 41)
7.   Cuspius Fadus (AD 44 – AD 46)
8.   Tiberius Alexander (AD 46 – AD 48)
9.   Ventidius Cumanus (AD 48 – AD 52)
10. Albinus (AD 61 – AD 65)

C.   EMPEROR CALIGULA (AD 37 – AD 41)

Caligula reigned from AD 37 to AD 41 (**4** years). At a certain time in the history of his reign, he suddenly developed a very wrong attitude of taking pleasure in being worshipped like the Almighty God. Thus, he proudly placed his statue or image in the Jerusalem Temple, and issued a decree that the Jews should worship him. Unfortunately, this demonic decree could not be carried out before he was eventually killed.

D.   EMPEROR CLAUDIUS (AD 41 – AD 54): ACTS 11:28; 18:2

Claudius Caesar ruled from AD 41 to AD 54 (**13** years). It was during his reign that most of Paul's preaching journeys were made.

Unfortunately, a civil disturbance broke out in Rome, and Emperor Claudius, blaming it on the innocent Jews living in Rome at that time; ordered that they should all be urgently driven out of Rome. Thus, this ugly incident affected **Aquila**, a Jew, who was also living in Rome with his wife, **Priscilla**. So they were left with no option than to leave Rome for Corinth (Acts 18:2):

> *"And found a certain Jew named **Aquila**, born in Pontus, lately come from Italy, with his wife **Priscilla**;*

(because that Claudius had commanded all Jews to depart from Rome:) and came unto them".

E.   KING HEROD AGRIPPA II (AD 50 – AD 70): ACTS 25:13-26:32

During the reign of Emperor Claudius in AD 50, Herod Agrippa II, son of Herod Agrippa I, and great-grand son of Herod the Great, whose sister was Bernice (Acts 25:13; 26:30), was appointed by the Roman authority to rule over the territory of his late father (Herod Agrippa I) as King (Acts 25:13-26:32). He ruled from AD 50 to AD 70, a period of twenty years. But he later died in AD 92.

F.   EMPEROR NERO (AD 54 – AD 68): ACTS 25:10-28:19

After the death of Claudius, Nero was appointed Emperor by the Roman Senate in AD 54. The name Nero is not clearly mentioned in the New Testament, but simply referred to as Caesar in Acts 25-28. He ruled from AD 54 to AD 68 (a period of **14** years).

During this period, he was known for ignorantly **persecuting** Jewish Christians within his territory.

It was this Emperor that Apostle Paul appealed to, as recorded in Acts chapter 25, and who was also responsible for killing Peter and Paul in the so-called **Nero persecution**. The effect of this persecution attracted the ***First Jewish Revolt*** in AD 66.

Sadly, he died in AD 68 by committing suicide, because he could not withstand the consequences of the upcoming Jewish Revolt:

1. The First Jewish Revolt (AD 66 - AD 70)

In AD 66, a terrible war broke out in Jerusalem between the Jews and the Roman government which was caused by some Jewish rebels *(zealots)*, and a lot of lives and property were mercilessly destroyed. *(**Note:** This war extended to AD 70 when Jerusalem and the Temple were destroyed).* In fact, the war took **4** years.

G. Emperor Vespasian (AD 69 – AD 79)

Vespasian had been a Roman military commander in Palestine from AD 66 to AD 69 (**3** years). After the death of Emperor Nero, he was made Emperor in AD 69, but officially appointed Emperor in AD 70 by the Roman Senate.

During this period, he mobilized the Roman army to suppress the first Jewish revolt that started in AD 66 by the powers of a Roman army general, and then committed the rest military battles to his eldest son, Titus. Thereafter, he returned to Rome to have his official appointment as an Emperor.

H. Emperor Titus (AD 79 – AD 81)

Emperor Titus was already an "associate Emperor" with his father Vespasian. So when his father finally returned to Rome for the official recognition, he succeeded him as the Emperor in AD 79, and then consequently led his army to destroy Jerusalem and the Temple in AD 70. *(Remember, this was the beautiful Temple that was built by Herod the Great during the first century AD, but completed many years after his death).* Emperor Titus finally died in AD 81.

Following the destruction, all Jewish Temple worship and sacrifices came to an end.

In the circumstance, not to allow their spiritual life waste away unnecessarily, some Jewish rabbis *(teachers)* decided to establish a school in the Mediterranean coastal town of "Jamnia *(Yavneh)*" so that they could have an opportunity to come together to study and explain the Torah or Old Testament Law of Moses *(Genesis to Deuteronomy).*

I. DOMITIAN (AD 81 – AD 96)

Upon the death of Emperor Titus, his younger brother Domitian succeeded him, because he had no son to succeed him on the throne.

Domitian displayed the worst type of an Emperor who had ever reigned in the Roman Empire, because he ruled with an evil heart! He was known for persecuting the Christian church during the period of his reign.

In AD 96, Emperor Domitian was successfully killed by a combined plan in the Empire.

It should be noted here that during the reign of Domitian, the Book of Revelation was also written.

J. THE SECOND JEWISH REVOLT (BEYOND AD 100): AD 132 - AD 135

After the first Jewish Revolt of AD 66 – AD 70, peace was not yet fully restored in Palestine, when unfortunately, Emperor Hadrian who ruled from AD 117 to AD 138, a period of **21** years, built an idol temple in the very location of the destroyed Jerusalem Temple and dedicated it to the Roman god *(Jupiter)*, in addition to other religious crimes against the Jews.

Thus, this devilish act of Emperor Hadrian caused the **Second Jewish Revolt** in AD 132, often referred to as the *"Bar Kochba's Revolt"*, which was bravely headed by **Simeon Bar Kosiba**, a supposed Messiah of the Jews.

In AD 135, the Roman authority successfully arrested the situation and brought it under full control. Jerusalem was then rebuilt by the Romans, but made it a pagan Roman City, thus preventing Jews to live in it.

The main reason behind this devilish act of the Roman authority, therefore, was nothing far from reducing the Jews to complete strangers in their own land and consequently humiliating them before the whole world.

CHAPTER III

RELIGIOUS BACKGROUND HISTORY OF THE NEW TESTAMENT BIBLE (FROM 539 BC TO 135 AD)

I. THE INTERTESTAMENTAL PERIOD (539 BC – 4 BC)

On the religious background, we shall be considering Israel's general religious activities during the intertestamental period that eventually caused the various religious disagreements and confusions between Jesus and the Jews, which took place in the New Testament Bible period. This will further strengthen our understanding of the real religious problems or situations in which the Jews later found themselves:

A. EFFECTS OF POLITICAL RULE ON JEWISH RELIGIOUS LIFE

1. The period of Ptolemaic Rule headed by Ptolemy

During the period of the Ptolemaic Rule in Palestine, Israel was given total freedom in matters concerning their religious worship and practices. The office of high priest was also set up and given necessary authority to handle both religious and civil matters affecting the Jews. The only thing that the Ptolemaic authority required from Israel was to pay a yearly tax to the authority.

Unfortunately, all this freedom came to an unnecessary end, when the Seleucid authority rose up against the Ptolemaic authority in a very serious military attack and successfully took over Palestine.

2. The period of Seleucid Rule headed by Seleucus

During the reign of the Seleucid Empire over Palestine, the Jews were seriously maltreated to the point that they were **denied all their religious rights**, including the office of high priest!

The Seleucid authority, in order to completely destroy Judaism (religion of the Jews), made every effort to stop the Jews from engaging in any religious activities.

For this reason, the authority polluted the Jewish Temple by sacrificing a pig on its altar, and then setting up a pagan altar in the Temple to the Greek god "**Zeus**".

In the circumstance, the Jews were forced to carry out immoral sexual activities in the Temple in worship of the Greek god; parents were no longer allowed to circumcise their male children; observance of the Sabbath Day was cancelled; a death sentence was placed on anyone who would be found to have in possession of a copy of the Law (Torah); etc.

To make matters worse still, the Seleucid authority sent army officers to every Jewish village to force them to offer sacrifice to **Zeus**, the Greek god.

On one of such occasions, an army officer was sent to Modein, a village not far from Jerusalem, to enforce the law on a Jewish Priest called Mattathias, to offer the ungodly sacrifice. But Mattathias, who was never afraid of the presence of the army officer, refused to offer the sacrifice; and a religiously disloyal Jew volunteered himself to do it. This unfaithful attitude of the Jew made Mattathias very angry, and consequently killed both the Jew and the army officer. Following this act of Priest Mattathias, therefore, a bloody war between the Maccabeans and the Seleucid authority broke out, which is often called the "**MACCABEAN REVOLT**"!

3. **The period of Maccabean Rule headed by Priest Mattathias**

During this period, the office of high priest was restored; religious worship and practices were given proper attention, as well as the cleansing and rededication of the Temple for the worship of Jehovah.

It was actually a period of self-government: a political, religious and cultural independence for the people of Israel.

4. **The period of Roman Rule headed by Herod the Great**

When Rome took over power from the Maccabeans, the Roman authority did not stop the Jews from carrying on with their religious activities.

In fact, the office of high priest as well as their religious worship and practices were maintained by the Roman authority.

The economic and social oppression that Rome gave to the Jews through King Herod the Great, was the demand for the payment of high tax and obedience to Roman laws.

B. INTERTESTAMENTAL JEWISH RELIGION (JUDIASM)

Despite all the religious problems that the Jews faced during the Intertestamental Period, the people of Israel truly devoted themselves to the study and application of the Law (Pentateuch or the 5 books of Moses: Genesis – Deuteronomy), in order to properly strengthen their spiritual relationship with Jehovah – their God. This renewed spiritual zeal led to the founding of different Jewish religious **sects** or **groups** like the Pharisees, Sadducees, Essenes, Zealots, Scribes, and Common People, as well as religious **institutions** like the Temple, Synagogue and Sanhedrin.

Historically, the Hasidaeans or Hasidim, that is, "*the group of Jews who supported the fight against Hellenism or Greek culture to gain religious freedom in Israel during the rule of the Greek Empire*", gave birth to the three main groups (Pharisees, Sadducees and Essenes), while Zealots as a group, was formed from both the Pharisees and Essenes.

Let us consider in a more detailed form, the nature and belief system of the religious sects or groups of Pharisees, Sadducees, Essenes, Zealots and Scribes:

1. Pharisees

    a. Their Nature

    The Pharisees were not the wealthy ones, but were just "middle-level businessmen". As a religious group, their main concern was how they could improve the spiritual life of the Jewish people with their God, in the areas of reading, teaching and practice of the Mosaic Law; fellowship, prayer, etc.

    Although, the Pharisees occupied minority seats out of the 70 seats in the **Sanhedrin** *(Jewish Supreme Court)*, yet they had greater influence on the decisions of the Court, because they gained majority support from the Jewish population.

    Religiously speaking, the Pharisees always separated themselves from those Jews termed **common people** (Mk 12:37): *that is, the general Jewish population that had not joined any Jewish religious group like the Pharisees, Sadducees, Essenes, Zealots and Scribes – they were regarded as being ignorant of the law and spiritually unclean*, so that they would not be defiled by their alleged religious impurities. The Pharisees, therefore, regarded these ignorant Jewish people as **sinners**.

The picture can be clearer when seen from Matt 9:10-13:

> *"And it came to pass, as Jesus sat at meat in the house, behold, many publicans and sinners came and sat down with him and his disciples. And when the Pharisees saw it, they said unto his disciples, Why eateth your Master with publicans and* **sinners***? But when Jesus heard that, he said unto them, They that be whole need not a physician, but they that are sick, But go ye and learn what that meaneth, I will have mercy, and not sacrifice: for I am not come to call the righteous, but* **sinners** *to repentance."*

Examples of Pharisees in the New Testament include: Saul (Paul), Nicodemus, Joseph of Arimathea, Gameliel, etc.

b. Their Beliefs

The Pharisees believed in the Torah or Law (the 5 books of Moses) as being divinely inspired by God. They also believed in Oral Tradition or Law. The Oral Law contains laws or traditions **allegedly** believed to have been given to Moses orally by God on Mount Sinai, as at the time God was giving him the Mosaic Law; which were not written down but memorized by Moses and then passed on to future generations *(from Moses to Joshua, to the Elders, to the Prophets, and then, to the Pharisees)*. According to the Pharisees, the Oral Law was as divinely inspired as that of the Written Law of God, and so had the same equal divine authority.

Their argument was that, the written Law could never be complete without the addition of the Oral Law, because it was the Oral Law that must be used in explaining the written Law for clearer understanding and application. Adding that without the Oral Law, it was very difficult to understand the written one. Thus, in an uncontrolled effort to apply principles of the Written Law to everyday living of the Jews, they ignorantly added their own mystical or spiritual interpretations, and styles of application to the written Law, as against the divine instruction of not **adding** or **subtracting** from the Written Word of God - Deut 4:2:

> *"Ye shall not **add** unto the word which I command you, neither shall ye **diminish** ought from it, that ye may keep the commandments of the LORD your God which I command you".*

It was because of this religious attitude of their *"rigorous and strict interpretation and observance of the Mosaic Law in both its oral and written form"*, that made Jesus to have serious doctrinal problems with them, and the so-called tradition of the elders that they had used carelessly in canceling certain aspects of the Written Word of God (Matt 15:6):

"And honour not his father or his mother, he shall be free. Thus have ye made the **commandment of God of none effect by your tradition.***"*

Theologically, the true fact is that, **wrong biblical interpretation leads to wrong biblical application, which also leads to wrong human behaviour.** And the Pharisees were completely guilty of this act.

The Pharisees believed that God is in full control of human affairs on earth, but also believed that one's personal right or wrong actions can help to shape his own destiny or future life.

In addition, they believed that at the end of the world, there would be resurrection for those that were already dead. And that God would definitely reward or punish everyone after this life.

Furthermore, they believed that there is a spirit world of angels and demons!

2. Sadducees

a. Their Nature

The Sadducees were the wealthiest and highly educated ones - they were of the *"upper-level of economic life."*

The group was well known in both political and religious affairs. **Politically**, they supported the Hellenistic (Greek) practices of the Roman government in Israel. And **religiously**, they were in-charge of the Temple activities which included: ritual sacrifices, priestly duties like chief priests and high priest, etc.

They occupied majority seats in the Sanhedrin, but lacked majority influence on the decisions of the Court, because they were not well respected or accepted by the Jewish population like their counterpart, the Pharisees. This is so, because they related well with **only** the wealthy, highly educated and politically influential people of their immediate society than the less-privileged of the Jewish population.

Examples of Sadducees in the New Testament were: Annas and Caiaphas, who were Jewish high priests.

b. Their Beliefs

The Sadducees did not believe in the Oral Law as against the belief of the Pharisees. They never believed in the fact that God controls human affairs on earth.

In addition, they did not believe in the resurrection of the dead or life after death, as well as existence of the spirit-world.

3. Essenes

a. Their Nature

The Essenes were a group of few Jews who decided to withdraw themselves from the general Jewish population in Jerusalem to found their own community near the Dead Sea. Their purpose was to separate themselves from the general people's spiritual pollution in the city into a perfect spiritual life and environment that is free from external spiritual pollutions, in order to prepare for the coming of God's Kingdom.

In their unreserved devotion to God, they strictly obeyed the provisions of the Written Law as given to Moses by God, as well as carrying out total self-discipline or self-punishment (asceticism) in order to attain spiritual holiness.

b. Their Beliefs

The Essenes believed in communalism or collectivism, that is, nobody in the community was allowed to own personal property. On the other hand, individual property of any kind was brought to the community's central store for the welfare of all members of the community.

They believed in manual labour. Everybody in the community was engaged in one form of labour like, agriculture or handicrafts.

On a general note, like the Pharisees, they believed in resurrection of the dead, life after death, as well as existence of the spirit world of angels and demons. In addition, they were expecting a Messiah who would be able to deliver Israel from the hands of Roman over-lordship to gain their spiritual freedom.

Notably, the Dead Sea Scrolls which were

essential to the completion of the Jewish Bible discovered in 1946 had been linked to them. This was made possible only, because of their strong belief in God and His sacred writings.

4. **Zealots**

   a. **Their Nature**

   Zealots were a group of Jews who became freedom fighters. According to them, Israel as a Theocratic nation (a nation ruled by God Himself), was supposed to have been ruled by priests under the leadership of Jehovah Himself. But surprisingly, they discovered that the pagan Roman military government had been ruling the Jews and with a lot of oppressive treatment.

   This ugly situation did not go down well with the Zealots, so they were moved to rise up against the Roman authority with weapons of war to force them out of the Holy Land and gain Independence for the Jews in order for the priests to rule the nation again under the divine leadership of Jehovah.

   The Zealots (*civilians*), should therefore be highly praised for their boldness in fighting against a well equipped military authority, because they never loved their lives. And of course, many did lose their lives in the struggle!

   New Testament examples of Zealots were: Simon the Zealot, a disciple who later became an apostle, as well as Barabbas, the freedom fighter.

b. Their Beliefs

Zealots believed in Jehovah as the **only** Jewish King who should rule Israel. And they never believed in the idea of any foreign pagan rulership over Israel.

5. Scribes

Scribes were a group of highly educated Jewish People involved in the safe-keeping of the ancient manuscripts of the Scriptures, especially the Mosaic Law.

Because there was a high demand for the knowledge and application of the Written Law by the people of Israel, the Scribes answered this call by being *"copyists* (since there was no printing machine in existence at that time), *editors, teachers and jurists."*

For the Scribes, the Mosaic Law was a better profession for them, so they gave in their time to be well educated in the **school** of the Law, and graduated to become doctors, teachers and lawyers of the Law. They were the experts of the Mosaic Law. In the Gospels of the New Testament Bible, they were often addressed as the doctors and teachers of the law.

C. Intertestamental Jewish Literature

During the Intertestamental period, a lot of biblical writings took place, which also shaped the New Testament biblical literature:

1. **Septuagint**

The word Septuagint is represented in Roman numbering system as "LXX", which is the English figure **70**. Septuagint, therefore, simply means the *"Greek translation of the Hebrew Scriptures."* It is commonly believed that *"72 Jewish scholars from Jerusalem"* were used for the work of translating the Hebrew Bible into Greek language in Egypt, on the request of Ptolemy II Philadelphia of Egypt, for the purpose of having *"a copy of the Hebrew Scriptures for the library in Alexandria."*

2. **Apocryphal**

These books are not found in the Jewish and Christian Bibles, but are included in the Roman Catholic Bible. They contain "history, fiction, and wisdom" writings:

    a. 1 Esdras
    b. 2 Esdras
    c. Tobit
    d. Judith
    e. Additions to the Book of Esther
    f. Wisdom of Solomon
    g. Sirach
    h. 1 Baruch
    i. Epistle of Jeremiah
    j. The Prayer of Azariah and the Song of the Three Young Men
    k. Susanna
    l. Bel and the Dragon
    m. The Prayer of Manassah

n.   1 Maccabees

o.   2 Maccabees

3. Pseudepigrapha

It is a collection of Jewish writings that is not contained in either the Jewish canon nor the Apocrypha:

   a.   Testament of the Twelve Patriarchs

   b.   Testament of Job

   c.   Martyrdom of Isaiah

   d.   3 and 4 Maccabees

   e.   Paralipomena of Jeremiah

   f.   Life of Adam and Eve

   g.   2 Baruch

   h.   3 Baruch

   i.   Psalms of Solomon

   j.   1 Enoch

   k.   2 Enoch

   l.   Assumption of Moses

   m. Letter of Aristeas

   n.   Sibulline Oracles

4. Dead Sea Scrolls

Scrolls of biblical Scriptures discovered in a cave near the Dead Sea in 1946.

5. Jewish Writers

During this period, a few Jewish historians and writers put their God-given writing talent into proper and effective use for the benefit of future generations. They wrote extensively on different Jewish religious matters and they have now become very important to theological research students, ministers of the gospel as well as Christians.

Two of such well known Jewish writers and historians were Philo "*(an Alexandrian Jew who wrote in Greek)*" and Flavius Josephus "*(a Palestinian Priest and Pharisee, and leader in the first Jewish revolt of AD 66 who also wrote in Greek).*"

6.   Rabbinical Literature

The Pharisees wrote down the Oral Law or tradition of the elders, as well as their own spiritual interpretations and styles of application of the Torah (the books of Moses); in what is known as **MISHNAH**, under the supervision of a Jewish Teacher – Judah.

Thus, the Mishnah is a major Jewish religious book that contains all about the oral law or tradition of the elders.

Apart from the Mishnah, there were other useful religious books written by the Pharisees on the Jewish Scriptures:

a.   Talmud

It contained the Hebrew version of the oral laws.

The Talmud had other supporting books. These were:

(1) Tosefta

It was a record of *"additions to the Mishnah."*

(2) Gemara

It was written in Aramaic language with two divisions:

- (a) **Halakah:** It had legal material relating to "613 additions to the Law".
- (b) **Haggadah:** It had parables and anecdotes from lives of famous rabbis.

b. Targum

The Targum was an Aramaic paraphrase of the Hebrew Bible.

c. Midrash

Midrash contained commentaries on the Hebrew biblical books.

II. THE GOSPEL PERIOD: 4 BC – AD 30 (MATT 2:1-JN 21)

A. JEWISH HIGH PRIESTS IN THE TIME OF JESUS

1. Annas (AD 6 – AD 15): Lk 3:2; Jn 18:13-14; Acts 4:6

Annas served as high priest in Jerusalem for **9** years, from AD 6 – AD 15. He was later removed from office by the Roman authority in AD 15.

Though legally removed from office, Annas was still whole-heartedly accepted and recognized by the

Jews as their respected high priest, this can be clearly seen from Jn 18:13:

> *"And led him away to **Annas** first; for he was father in law to Caiaphas, which was the high priest that same year".*

> **Acts 4:6** *"And **Annas** the high priest, and Caiaphas, and John, and Alexander, and as many as were of the kindred of the high priest, were gathered together at Jerusalem".*

2. **Caiaphas (Son-in-law to Annas): AD 18 – AD 36 (Matt 26:3; Mk 14:53-72; 15:1-15; Lk 3:2; Jn 11:49, 57; 18:13, 28; Acts 4:6; 5:17; Jas 5:12)**

Caiaphas was appointed high priest in AD 18 by the Roman authority during the reign of Tiberius Caesar and reigned till AD 36 (**18** years):

> **Lk 3:2** *"Annas and **Caiaphas** being the high priests, the word of God came unto John the son of Zacharias in the wilderness". He was a son-in-law to Annas (Jn 18:13), the former high priest, politically speaking!*

It was Caiaphas who made the statement in Jn 11:50 *"it is expedient for us, that one man should die for the people, and that the whole nation perish not".*

Jesus was arrested and brought first to Annas *(former high priest)*, and then taken to Caiaphas *(the present high priest)*, for proper trial (Matt 26:57-68; Mk 14:53-72; Lk 22:54-71; Jn 18:13-27).

At the end of the trial, Jesus was consequently condemned to death by the Jewish authority under the leadership of Caiaphas, the high priest. This unanimous condemnation of Jesus further gave full rights to the Jews over Jesus to spit on His face, get Him beaten and pour insulting statements on Him (Matt 26:67-68):

> "Then did they **spit in his face**, and **buffeted** him; and others **smote** him with the palms of their hands, Saying, Prophesy unto us, thou Christ, Who is he that smote thee?".

In the circumstance, Caiaphas being a high priest, had no political or judicial powers to pass death sentence on Jesus, so Jesus was sent to Pilate, the Roman governor at that time, who had the legal powers to confirm, declare and subsequently carry out the necessary death sentence on Jesus (Jn 18:28-19:16):

> "And the servants and officers stood there, who had made a fire of coals; for it was cold: and they warmed themselves: and Peter stood with them, and warmed himself. The high priest then asked Jesus of his disciples, and of his doctrine. Jesus answered him, I spake openly to the world; I ever taught in the synagogue, and in the temple, whither the Jews always resort; and in secret have I said nothing. Why askest thou me? ask them which heard me, what I have said unto them: behold, they know what I said. And when he had thus spoken, one

of the officers which stood by struck Jesus with the palm of his hand, saying, Answerest thou the high priest so? Jesus answered him, If I have spoken evil, bear witness of the evil: but if well, why smitest thou me? Now Annas had sent him bound unto Caiaphas the high priest. And Simon Peter stood and warmed himself. They said therefore unto him, Art not thou also one of his disciples? He denied it, and said, I am not. One of the servants of the high priest, being his kinsman whose ear Peter cut off, saith, Did not I see thee in the garden with him? Peter then denied again: and immediately the cock crew. Then led they Jesus from Caiaphas unto the hall of judgment: and it was early; and they themselves went not into the judgment hall, lest they should be defiled; but that they might eat the passover. Pilate then went out unto them, and said, What accusation bring ye against this man? They answered and said unto him, If he were not a malefactor, we would not have delivered him up unto thee. Then said Pilate unto them, Take ye him, and judge him according to your law. The Jews therefore said unto him, It is not lawful for us to put any man to death: That the saying of Jesus might be fulfilled, which he spake, signifying what death he should die. Then Pilate entered into the judgment hall again, and called Jesus, and said unto him, Art thou the King of the Jews? Jesus answered him, Sayest thou this thing of thyself, or did others tell it thee of me? Pilate answered, Am I a Jew? Thine own nation and the chief priests have delivered thee *unto me: what hast thou done? Jesus answered, My kingdom is not of this world: if my kingdom were of this world, then would my servants fight, that I should not be delivered to the Jews: but now is my kingdom not from hence. Pilate therefore said unto him, Art thou a king then? Jesus answered, Thou sayest that I am a king. To this end was I born, and for this cause came I into the world, that I should bear witness unto the truth. Every one that is of the truth heareth my voice. Pilate saith unto him, What is truth? And when he had said this, he went out again unto the Jews, and saith unto them, I find in him no fault at all. But ye have a custom, that I should release unto you one at the passover: will ye therefore that I release unto you the King of the Jews? Then cried they all again, saying, Not this man, but **Barabbas**. Now Barabbas was a robber. Then Pilate therefore took Jesus, and scourged him. And the soldiers platted a crown of thorns, and put it on his head, and they put on him a purple robe, And said, Hail, King of the Jews! and they smote him with their hands. Pilate therefore went forth again, and saith unto them, Behold, I bring him forth to you, that ye may know that I find no fault in him Then came Jesus forth, wearing the crown of thorns, and the purple robe. And Pilate saith unto them, Behold the man! When the chief priests therefore and officers saw him, they cried out, saying, Crucify him, crucify him. Pilate saith unto them, Take ye him, and crucify him: for I find no fault in him. The Jews answered him,*

We have a law, and by our law he ought to die, because he made himself the Son of God. When Pilate therefore heard that saying, he was the more afraid; And went again into the judgment hall, and saith unto Jesus, Whence art thou? But Jesus gave him no answer. Then saith Pilate unto him, Speakest thou not unto me? knowest thou not that I have power to crucify thee, and have power to release thee? Jesus answered, Thou couldest have no power at all against me, except it were given thee from above: therefore he that delivered me unto thee hath the greater sin. And from thenceforth Pilate sought to release him: but the Jews cried out, saying, If thou let this man go, thou art not Caesar's friend: whosoever maketh himself a king speaketh against Caesar. When Pilate therefore heard that saying, he brought Jesus forth, and sat down in the judgment seat in a place that is called the Pavement, but in the Hebrew, Gabbatha. And it was the preparation of the passover, and about the sixth hour: and he saith unto the Jews, Behold your King! But they cried out, Away with him, away with him, crucify him. Pilate saith unto them, Shall I crucify your King? The chief priests answered, We have no king but Caesar. Then delivered he him therefore unto them to be crucified. And they took Jesus, and led him away".

In reference to the above Scriptural passage, I wish to quickly point out here, that **Barabbas** was never a robber in the criminal sense, but simply a leader of a group of freedom fighters (*Zealots*), who was **only** fighting for Jewish political freedom from Roman political slavery. So it was not funny for the Jews to have demanded for the release of the **good man** (*Barabbas*), who was totally committed to fighting for their political freedom (Mk 15:6-15):

> *"Now at that feast he released unto them one prisoner, whomsoever they desired. And there was one named **Barabbas**, which lay bound with them that had made **insurrection** with him, who had committed murder in the insurrection. And the multitude crying aloud began to desire him to do as he had ever done unto them. But Pilate answered them, saying, Will ye that I release unto you the King of the Jews? For he knew that the chief priests had delivered him for envy. But the chief priests moved the people, that he should rather release Barabbas unto them. And Pilate answered and said again unto them, What will ye then that I shall do unto him whom ye call the King of the Jews? And they cried out again, Crucify him. Then Pilate said unto them, Why, what evil hath he done? And they cried out the more exceedingly, Crucify him. And so Pilate, willing to content the people, released Barabbas unto them, and delivered Jesus, when he had scourged him, to be crucified".*

> **Lk 23:17-19** *"(For of necessity he must release one unto them at the feast.) And they cried out all at once, saying, Away with this man, and release unto us **Barabbas**: (Who for a certain sedition made in the city, and for murder, was cast into prison".*

Caiaphas developed a very great hatred against the Person of Christ. As a result, this hatred was further directed at the apostles of Christ in the form of severe persecution as revealed in Acts 4:1-22:

"And as they spake unto the people, the priests, and the captain of the temple, and the Sadducees, came upon them, Being grieved that they taught the people, and preached through Jesus the resurrection from the dead. And they laid hands on them, and put them in hold unto the next day: for it was now eventide. Howbeit many of them which heard the word believed; and the number of the men was about five thousand. And it came to pass on the morrow, that their rulers, and elders, and scribes, And Annas the high priest, and Caiaphas, and John, and Alexander, and as many as were of the kindred of the high priest, were gathered together at Jerusalem. And when they had set them in the midst, they asked, By what power, or by what name, have ye done this? Then Peter, filled with the Holy Ghost, said unto them, Ye rulers of the people, and elders of Israel, If we this day be examined of the good deed done to the impotent man, by what means he is made whole; Be it known unto you all, and to all the people of Israel, that by the name of Jesus Christ of Nazareth, whom ye crucified, whom God raised from the dead, even by him doth this man stand here before you whole. This is the stone which was set at nought of you builders, which is become the head of the corner. Neither is there salvation in any other: for there is none other name

under heaven given among men, whereby we must be saved. Now when they saw the boldness of Peter and John, and perceived that they were unlearned and ignorant men, they marvelled; and they took knowledge of them, that they had been with Jesus. And beholding the man which was healed standing with them, they could say nothing against it. But when they had commanded them to go aside out of the council, they conferred among themselves, Saying, What shall we do to these men? for that indeed a notable miracle hath been done by them is manifest to all them that dwell in Jerusalem; and we cannot deny it. But that it spread no further among the people, let us straitly threaten them, that they speak henceforth to no man in this name. And they called them, and commanded them not to speak at all nor teach in the name of Jesus. But Peter and John answered and said unto them, Whether it be right in the sight of God to hearken unto you more than unto God, judge ye. For we cannot but speak the things which we have seen and heard. So when they had further threatened them, they let them go, finding nothing how they might punish them, because of the people: for all men glorified God for that which was done. For the man was above forty years old, on whom this miracle of healing was shewed".

Acts 5:17-42 *"Then the high priest rose up, and all they that were with him, and were filled with indignation, And laid their hands on the apostles, and put them in the common prison. But the angel* of the Lord by night opened the prison doors, and brought them forth, and said, Go, stand and speak in the temple to the people all the words of this life. And when they heard that, they entered into the temple early in the morning, and taught. But the high priest came, and they that were with him, and called the council together, and all the senate of the children of Israel, and sent to the prison to have them brought. But when the officers came, and found them not in the prison, they returned, and told, Saying, The prison truly found we shut with all safety, and the keepers standing without before the doors: but when we had opened, we found no man within. Now when the high priest and the captain of the temple and the chief priests heard these things, they doubted of them whereunto this would grow. Then came one and told them, saying, Behold, the men whom ye put in prison are standing in the temple, and teaching the people. Then went the captain with the officers, and brought them without violence: for they feared the people, lest they should have been stoned. And when they had brought them, they set them before the council: and the high priest asked them, Saying, Did not we straitly command you that ye should not teach in this name? and, behold, ye have filled Jerusalem with your doctrine, and intend to bring this man's blood upon us. Then Peter and the other apostles answered and said, We ought to obey God rather than men. The God of our fathers raised up Jesus, whom ye slew and hanged on a tree. Him hath

God exalted with his right hand to be a Prince and a Saviour, for to give repentance to Israel, and forgiveness of sins. And we are his witnesses of these things; and so is also the Holy Ghost, whom God hath given to them that obey him. When they heard that, they were cut to the heart, and took counsel to slay them. Then stood there up one in the council, a Pharisee, named Gamaliel, a doctor of the law, had in reputation among all the people, and commanded to put the apostles forth a little space; And said unto them, Ye men of Israel, take heed to yourselves what ye intend to do as touching these men. For before these days rose up Theudas, boasting himself to be somebody; to whom a number of men, about four hundred, joined themselves: who was slain; and all, as many as obeyed him, were scattered, and brought to nought. After this man rose up Judas of Galilee in the days of the taxing, and drew away much people after him: he also perished; and all, even as many as obeyed him, were dispersed. And now I say unto you, Refrain from these men, and let them alone: for if this counsel or this work be of men, it will come to nought: But if it be of God, ye cannot overthrow it; lest haply ye be found even to fight against God. And to him they agreed: and when they had called the apostles, and beaten them, they commanded that they should not speak in the name of Jesus, and let them go. And they departed from the presence of the council, rejoicing that they were counted worthy to suffer shame for his name. And daily in the temple, and in every house, they ceased not to teach and preach Jesus Christ".

In addition, he also presided over the trial of Peter in Acts 4:6 *"And Annas the high priest, and Caiaphas, and John, and Alexander, and as many as were of the kindred of the high priest, were gathered together at Jerusalem".*

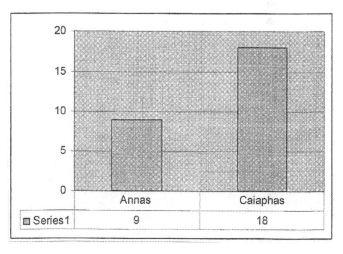

Years of reign of the two high priests

B. JEWISH MIS-DIRECTED MESSIANIC EXPECTATION

Because of the bitter political, religious and cultural experiences that the Jews went through in the hands of different pagan world powers, at the time of Christ, their messianic expectation had completely changed from that of a true *Spiritual Messiah* who should save them from a national spiritual bondage of sin; to a supposed

Political Messiah who would come to deliver them from the political bondage of the Roman Empire.

This wrong messianic expectation was the reason why the Jews *(Scribes, Pharisees, Sadducees, Chief Priests and Elders)*, could not accept Jesus as their awaited Messiah, just because He refused to involve Himself in any form of political movement that would deliver them from their present political bondage to the Roman authority. But they never knew that Jesus came as a Spiritual Messiah to deliver them from the bondage of sin (Matt. 1:21):

> *"And she shall bring forth a son, and thou shalt call his name JESUS:* **for he shall save his people from their sins***"). They missed Him, and they missed it all!*

C. TEMPLE WORSHIP

It was the custom of the Jews to travel to Jerusalem three times a year to offer ritual sacrifices according to the Jewish sacrificial feasts of "**Passover**", "**Sukkot**", and "**Shavuot**" as contained in the Torah. Jesus also attended several Passover celebrations during His ministry on earth.

D. THE SYNAGOGUE

At the time of Jesus, the Jews had already established synagogues almost in every city within the Roman Empire. Jesus was often seen going to the synagogue for the customary or usual reading of the Jewish Old Testament Scriptures.

E. TRADITION OF THE ELDERS

The Pharisees and Scribes were still very much alive with the usual practice of the oral law or tradition of the elders, along with the Torah, even in the time of Jesus:

> **Matt. 15:1-2** *"Then came to Jesus* **scribes** *and* **Pharisees***, which were of Jerusalem, saying, Why do thy disciples transgress the* **tradition of the elders***? for they wash not their hands when they eat bread".*

> **Mk 7:1-5** *"Then came together unto him the* **Pharisees***, and certain of the* **scribes***, which came from Jerusalem. And when they saw some of his disciples eat bread with defiled, that is to say, with unwashen, hands, they found fault. For the Pharisees, and all the Jews, except they wash their hands oft, eat not, holding the* **tradition of the elders***. And when they come from the market, except they wash, they eat not. And many other things there be, which they have received to hold, as the washing of cups, and pots, brasen vessels, and of tables. Then the* **Pharisees** *and* **scribes** *asked him, Why walk not thy disciples according to the* **tradition of the elders***, but eat bread with unwashen hands?"*

Biblically speaking, it was due to Jewish bad hermeneutics or application of wrong principles of biblical interpretation, which gave birth to the problem of "tradition of the elders", that we find in the Gospels of the New Testament Bible.

F. ROMAN RELIGION

During the time of Jesus, the Roman authority did not force their religion on the Jews, but they were allowed to go on with their Judaist belief; despite the fact that the Romans believed and worshipped many gods like: "Jupiter, Mercury, Venus, Hera, Apolo, Isis, Mithraism, and Cybele".

It was the Roman's custom to throw wild party which often involved *"drunkenness and open sexual intercourse"*, in worship of these gods.

It is worthy of note here that, the major religious influence that was in the center of attention during the Gospel Period in Palestine (Israel), was the Jewish Religion, which is Judaism.

From biblical evidence, you will agree with me that the Gospel Ministry of Christ was within the territory of Palestine or Israel. This therefore, speaks in favour of the practice of Judaism in Israel at the time of Christ's earthly ministry.

In fact, Jesus was born and grew up as a Jew, practised Judaism as His religion, preached and taught as a Jew to a Jewish audience. So from all points, He was completely Jewish in nature.

III. THE CHURCH PERIOD (AD 30 – AD 100)

A. JEWISH HIGH PRIEST IN THE TIME OF THE EARLY CHURCH

1. Ananias (AD 47 – AD 59): Acts 22:5, 12, 30; 23:1-5; 24:1

Ananias was a high priest of the Jews from AD 47 – AD 59, a period of **12** years.

During this period, Paul was falsely accused and arrested by the Jews and then brought before him *(Annanias)* and the Sanhedrin *(the Jewish Supreme Council)*, because of his gospel activities.

In defending himself, Paul made it very clear to the Council members in Acts 23:1 that he had done nothing wrong legally or religiously to have been arrested by the Jews, "*I have lived in all good conscience before God until this day.*" On hearing this statement of Paul, the high priest, Ananias, was unnecessarily angry and then ordered one of his personal assistants to slap Paul's mouth for making such supposed insulting statement.

In the circumstance, Paul, knowing fully well that he had never made any deliberate insulting statement about any particular member of the Council which could have attracted such deadly slap from the high priest; moved with a holy anger, and consequently pronounced a divine judgment on Ananias as recorded in Acts 23:1-3:

> *And Paul, earnestly beholding the council, said, Men and brethren, I have lived in all good*

conscience before God until this day. And the high priest Ananias commanded them that stood by him to smite him on the mouth. **Then said Paul unto him, God shall smite thee,** *thou whited wall: for sittest thou to judge me after the law, and commandest me to be smitten contrary to the law?*

Historically, in fulfillment of Paul's prophetic judgment on Ananias, just at the very beginning of the Second Jewish Revolt or War that took place in AD 66, when Jerusalem was being captured by the Romans, Ananias was brutally and mercilessly killed in the process.

B. JUDAISM AND CHRISTIANITY (AD 30-AD 100)

Christianity was established on the day of **Pentecost** *(a Jewish feast – Ex 23:16; 34:22; Lev 23:15-16; Num 28:26; Acts 2:1; 20:16; I Cor 16:8)*, and began to develop from that point.

For any religion to be practiced in the Roman Empire within this time, it must first be approved by the authority. Thus, Judaism was already an approved religion in the Empire. So, when Christianity first came into existence, it was regarded as a baby of Judaism. But when it grew to become a separate religion from Judaism, it was now punishable by death to practice it within the Empire, since it was not recognized or approved by the Roman authority.

This was the reason why the Apostles at that time were often arrested, as they preached the gospel of Christ and were brought before the Sanhedrin and the Roman authority for the **only** purpose of severe disciplinary action (Acts 4:1-31; 5:14-49).

C. EMPEROR WORSHIP (I COR 8:6, 12:2-3; REV 2:13;17:14)

Within the Roman Empire, **Emperor Worship** was set up; this was as a result of making the Emperor a divine being, which is like a **god**!

For this reason, it was made compulsory for all people within the Empire to take *"oath of allegiance"* making sure that they would ever remain loyal and obedient to the authority of the *Emperor, his children, as well as those of his family lineage after him*, in everything no matter the cost.

Acting on the authority of this **oath**, therefore, the Jews began to arrest the Apostles for preaching in the Name of Jesus Christ and brought them before the local magistrate's court on the accusation that they were being ***disloyal*** to the emperor (Acts 17:7):

> *"Whom Jason hath received:* **and these all do contrary to the decrees of Caesar, saying that there is another king, one Jesus"**.

D. GRECO-ROMAN RELIGION

The worship of Greco-Roman gods in the Roman Empire became very strong in this period.

These gods included:

1. Artemis (also known as Diana): Paul had an encounter with this goddess in Ephesus (Acts 19:24). Compare I Tim 2:11-15.

2. Zeus (Also known as Jupiter – Acts 14:12)
3. Hermes (Also known as Mercury or Mercurius - Acts 14:12)
4. Etc

E. PHILOSOPHICAL SCHOOLS

The practice of human idea of life or worldview, which is philosophical speculations, was also very common in this period:

1. Gnosticism

This is a Greek human idea of life and the world, which says that the physical human body is evil, but the spirit is good. For this reason, they strongly believed that Jesus did not come in human flesh or body as generally believed; and that it was only a foolish idea for anyone to ever believe in such an event.

But the New Testament Scriptures strongly opposed to all forms of this human idea or philosophy:

Col 2:8 *"Beware lest any man spoil you through **philosophy** and vain deceit, after the tradition of men, after the rudiments of the world, and not after Christ."*

I Tim 6:20 *"O Timothy, keep that which is committed to they trust, avoiding **profane** and **vain babblings**, and **oppositions of science** falsely so called"*

I Jn 4:1-3 *"Beloved, believe not every spirit, but try the spirits whether they are of God: because many false prophets are gone out into the world. Hereby know ye the Spirit of God: Every spirit that confesseth that **Jesus Christ is come in the flesh** is of God: And every spirit that confesseth not that **Jesus Christ is come in the flesh** is not of God: and this is that spirit of antichrist, whereof ye have heard that it should come; and even now already is it in the world."*

2. Stoicism and Epicureanism

   a. Stoicism

   This is also a Greek idea of the world, that it was created with a purpose, and that everybody had a personal responsibility to find out that purpose for himself, and then work accordingly in order to achieve it in his personal life.

   b. Epicureanism (Acts 17:18)

   Epicureanism as a Greek philosophy of life and the world says that the world was never created by any Supreme Being, but that it automatically came into existence.

   For this reason, the philosophy favours the fact that there is nothing anybody would ever desire to have in this world than to enjoy himself. According to this idea, there is only enjoyment and nothing else for anyone to look for in this life.

   In one of his missionary journeys, Paul had an encounter with these philosophers of **Stoicism** and **Epicureanism** in the city of Athens (Acts 17:18):

> *"Then certain philosophers of the **Epicureans** and the **Stoicks**, encountered him. And some said, What will this babbler say? Other some, He seemeth to be a setter forth of strange gods: because he preached unto them Jesus, and the resurrection."*

CHAPTER IV

CULTURAL BACKGROUND HISTORY OF THE NEW TESTAMENT BIBLE (FROM 539 BC TO 135 AD)

The New Testament cultural background is influenced by three main cultures, which are Jewish, Greek and Roman cultures.

However, because of some cultural fine-tuning made by the Roman administrators in respect of Greek and Roman cultures, the New Testament Bible, therefore, has come to have only two main cultural backgrounds: Jewish and Greco-Roman cultures.

In simple explanation, it was Alexander the Great of the Greek Empire that first introduced Greek culture in Israel, followed by the Seleucid Kingdom after his death. Then, when the Roman Empire took over Israel's political affairs, she continued with Greek cultural practices as well, from the Intertestamental period down to the end of the Book of Revelation.

Thus, Greek cultural practices were mixed together with Roman cultural practices by the Roman political administration, which in effect produced a Greco-Roman cultural background of the New Testament – Matthew to Revelation.

I. THE INTERTESTAMENTAL PERIOD (539 BC – 4 BC)

Here we shall briefly examine the cultural effects that the Persian, Greek and Roman Empires had on the Jews during this period:

1. THE PERSIAN EMPIRE

During the Persian rule, Aramaic became the official and main language of the Empire. To this end, the Jews adopted this language for their official business and inter-regional trade.

However, the Persian authority was very considerate and allowed the Jews to practice their own culture.

2. THE GREEK EMPIRE

With the coming of the Greek Empire, Greek language became the official and main language of the Empire. In addition, Greek cultural issues relating to religion, philosophy, currency and education were essentially maintained by the Empire.

On the other hand, Alexander the Great lovingly allowed the Jews to continue with their cultural practices. This same grace was upon the Jews during the Ptolemaic rule.

But under the Seleucid rule, the Jews were forced to obey the Greek culture to the letter. This cultural slavery led to the Jewish revolt in the Intertestamental period.

3. THE ROMAN EMPIRE

During this period, the Roman authority adopted a three-fold ***Hebrew-Greek-Roman*** cultural development plan within the Empire which greatly affected the Jewish cultural life.

II. The Gospel Period: 4 BC – AD 30 (MATT 2:1-JN 21)

A. Living Standard of the Jews

Most Jews were very poor because of the high tax payment introduced by the Roman government through Herod the Great. The Sadducees were the only people who were rich or wealthy, because they charged them high prices for their sacrificial animals and engaged in the lucrative money-changing business, since they were the ones in-charge of the Temple duties.

This ungodly attitude of the Sadducees in turning the Temple of God into a business centre instead of a place of worship was totally unacceptable to Jesus. Thus, He was forced to display His holy anger against this ugly development during His triumphal entry into Jerusalem and subsequent visit to the Temple (Matt. 21:12-13):

> *"And Jesus went into the temple of God, and cast out **all them that sold and bought in the temple**, and overthrew the tables of the **moneychangers**, and the seats of them that **sold doves**, And said unto them, It is written, My house shall be called the house of prayer; but ye have made it a den of thieves".*

B. Language

The Greek language was the general language (*lingua franca*) which was spoken all over the Roman Empire. No doubt, this development therefore, created an open door for the New Testament Scriptures to be written in the Greek language, which equally made it possible for many people in the Empire to have direct assess to the Scriptures in the Greek language.

On the other hand, Aramaic was used by the Jews in their everyday communication among themselves. Jesus also used Aramaic language in His communication with the Jews, since He was a Jew Himself. But Hebrew language was used for the reading of the Torah.

C. Education

Only Jewish male children were given the right to education, usually in the Torah. Their female counterparts were denied such right, simply considering them as the educationally less-privileged ones.

III. The Church Period (AD 30 – AD 100)

A. Slavery

The Roman authority instituted slavery, and it became one of their best institutions in the Empire. Statistically, slaves was said to have occupied approximately "60%" of the Roman world in biblical times!

No slave was ever given any fundamental human rights. They were often treated as mere human tools. In case of maltreatment, their masters were never cautioned or punished; rather they were given total freedom over their slaves by the Roman authority – compare Eph. 6:5-9:

"Servants, be obedient to them that are your masters according to the flesh, with fear and trembling, in singleness of your heart, as unto Christ; Not with eyeservice, as menpleasers; but as the servants of Christ, doing the will of God from the heart;".

CHAPTER V

RECOMMENDATION

Political, Religious and Cultural Background History of the New Testament Bible, is the first in the series of books on the New Testament background.

Therefore, I encourage all readers and students of the Bible to make sure that they get copy each of the books in the series, to enable them have an all-round knowledge of the New Testament Bible background. This will no doubt, place them in a better position to confidently read, study, interpret and apply the New Testament Scripture according to its original content and intent, *that is, according to the **original meaning** of its message to the **original receivers**, in the First Century.*

The list of books in the series includes the following:

1. Danger of "Tradition of the Elders" to New Testament Bible Interpretation

2. First Century Christianity in the New Testament Bible

3. First Century Greco-Roman Religion in the New Testament Bible

4. First Century Greco-Roman Culture in the New Testament Bible

5. Biblical Background of the New Testament Bible

7. First Century Roman Empire in New Testament Bible History

8. Historical Background of New Testament Bible Books

9. Christ's Prophetic Life in New Testament Revelation

Interested persons can contact me on any of the following GSM numbers: +2347033213028, +2347088585247.

BIBLIOGRAPHY

INTERTESTAMENTAL POLITICAL BACKGROUND HISTORY

History: Intertestamental - Bible History Links (Ancient Biblical ... www.bible-history.com/links.php?cat=14&sub...

Intertestamental History: myredeemer.exactpages.com/ ITHistoryp1.html

10. Intertestamental History: koinonia-all.org/bible/Intertestament. htm

[PDF] Messianic Expectations: markmoore.org/resources/essays/ loc/intertestamental.pdf

[PPT] BB 102-03: www.montreat.edu/dglassford/BB_102/.../ Class%20Three.ppt

[PDF] In What Ways Does a Knowledge of Intertestamental History and ... www.lastseminary.com/.../

Judaism History pdf | Download Free Judaism History Ebook www.lexiology.com/judaism-history.pdf - United States

Intertestamental period - CreationWiki, the encyclopedia of ...
creationwiki.org/Intertestamental_period
ad Dei Gloriam Ministries Bible Overview:
www.addeigloriam.org/bible-study-guide/bible-overview.htm

[PDF] Telling the New Testament Story of God:
www.nazarenepastor.org/clergyeducation/portals/0/.../NT_
StuGu.pdf

Peter's Burg: A Review of J. Julius Scott's "Jewish Backgrounds of ...
petermalik.blogspot.com/.../review-of-j-julius-scotts-jewish.
html

Intertestamental : Political History Of Levant
www.museumstuff.com/.../Intertestamental::sub::Political
_History_Of_Levant

*[DOC] Intertestamental History Collection of Essays - Welcome
to Groben.Com* www.groben.com/files/teachings/.../ID101%20
final%20exam%20Groben.doc

Babylonian Empire

www.livius.org/ba-bd/babylon/babylonian_empire.html
en.wikipedia.org/wiki/Babylonia
en.wikipedia.org/wiki/Neo-Babylonian_Empire
www.newworldencyclopedia.org/entry/Babylonian_
Empire
www.keyway.ca/htm2000/20000214.htm
www.bible-history.com/.../map_babylonian_empire_550_
bc.html
atheism.about.com/library/.../bldef_babylonianempire.
htm
www.ebibleteacher.com/batlasweb/sld028.htm
www.bartleby.com › HG Wells › A Short History of the World

Persian Empire

ancienthistory.about.com/od/iranmaps/qt/PersianEmpire.
htm
www.thebritishmuseum.ac.uk/forgottenempire/
www.thebritishmuseum.ac.uk/forgottenempire/
archaeology.about.com/.../persianempire/Ancient_Persian_
Empire.htm
en.wikipedia.org/wiki/Achaemenid_Empire
www.buzzle.com/articles/persian-empire.html
www.parstimes.com/.../brief_history_of_persian_empire.
html
www.jewishvirtuallibrary.org/jsource/History/Persians.
html

Greek Empire

en.wikipedia.org/wiki/Greek_Empire
en.wikipedia.org/wiki/Ancient_Greece
www.purposeinlife.org/series2/midi/7.5_The_Greek_Empire.
html
www.simpletoremember.com/articles/a/the_greek_
empire/
www.greeka.com/ancient-greece.htm
www.aish.com/jl/h/48939587.html

Alexander The Great

en.wikipedia.org/wiki/Alexander_the_Great
www.historyofmacedonia.org/.../AlexandertheGreat.
html
1stmuse.com/

INTERTESTAMENTAL RELIGIOUS BACKGROUND HISTORY

[PDF] THE STRANDS OF WISDOM TRADITION IN INTERTESTAMENTAL JUDAISM:
www.saiacs.org/.../BENNEMA-2001%20Tyndale%20Bulletin.pdf

[PDF] Intertestamental History
www.bju.edu/library/research-helps/.../intertestamental-history.pdf

Intertestamental Judaism - Associated Content from Yahoo ...
www.associatedcontent.com/article/.../intertestamental_judaism.html

[PDF] CONFRONTING THE SOURCES: THE INTERTESTAMENTAL PERIOD
rivkinsociety.com/documents/.../Confronting%20The%20Sources.pdf

[PDF] Intertestamental Judaism, its literature and its significance:
s3.amazonaws.com/tgc-documents/journal.../15.3_Beckwith.pdf

Web Directory: Judaism: www.bible-researcher.com › Web Directory
[PDF] ON THE VALUE OF INTERTESTAMENTAL JEWISH LITERATURE FOR NEW ...
www.etsjets.org/files/JETS-PDFs/23/23-4/23-4-pp315-323_JETS.pdf

[PDF] "The Challenge of Narrative Criticism to Background Studies":
journalofbiblicalstudies.org/Issue12/Nelson_Canonical_Criticism.pdf

[PDF] Lectures 3-4; Intertestamental Judaism.mell: homepage.mac.com/johnalex1/shelton/newtestament/lectures3-4.pdf

The Beliefs of the Pharisees, Sadducees, and Essenes : Chris ...
www.chris-sanchez.com/.../beliefs-of-pharisees-sadducees-and.
html

Pharisees - Wikipedia, the free encyclopedia: en.wikipedia.org/
wiki/Pharisees

Pharisees, Sadducees, and Essenes: www.jewishvirtuallibrary.
org/.../sadducees_pharisees_essenes.html

CATHOLIC ENCYCLOPEDIA: Pharisees:
www.newadvent.org › Catholic Encyclopedia › P

Daily Bible Study - Who Were The Pharisees?: www.keyway.ca/
htm2002/pharisee.htm

JewishEncyclopedia.com – PHARISEES: www.jewishencyclopedia.
com/view.jsp?artid=252&letter
Pharisees: mb-soft.com/believe/txc/pharisee.htm

Who were the Sadducees and the Pharisees?
www.gotquestions.org/Sadducees-Pharisees.html

Pharisees (WebBible™ Encyclopedia) - ChristianAnswers.Net
www.christiananswers.net/dictionary/pharisees.html

Jesus and the Pharisees:
www.bible-history.com/pharisees/PHARISEESJesus_and_the_
Pharisees.htm

Pharisees - Answers.com: www.answers.com › ... › Literature &
Language › Dictionary

Pharisees - LookLex Encyclopaedia: lexicorient.com/e.o/pharisees.
htm

Pharisees and Sadducees - Here a little, there a little – Commentary: www.herealittletherealittle.net/index.cfm?page...Pharisees...

Bible Encyclopedia: Pharisees: bibleencyclopedia.com/pharisees.htm

Pharisee (Jewish history) -- Britannica Online Encyclopedia www.britannica.com/EBchecked/topic/455129/Pharisee

Pharisees & Sadducees: virtualreligion.net/iho/pharisee.html

Pharisee – OrthodoxWiki: orthodoxwiki.org › Categories › Church History › Judaism

Matthew 23 - Religion Like the Pharisees: www.bible.ca/ef/expository-matthew-23.htm

Pharisees: latter-rain.com/gospel/phari.htm

Pharisees and Sadducees: gardenofpraise.com/bibl45s.htm

Pharisees - LoveToKnow 1911: www.1911encyclopedia.org/ Pharisees

Sadducees - Wikipedia, the free encyclopedia: en.wikipedia.org/ wiki/Sadducees

Sadducees: www.livius.org/saa-san/sadducees/sadducees.html

JewishEncyclopedia.com – SADDUCEES: www.jewishencyclopedia.com/view.jsp?artid=40&letter=S

Sadducees: mb-soft.com/believe/txo/sadducee.htm

CATHOLIC ENCYCLOPEDIA: Sadducees: www.newadvent.org › Catholic Encyclopedia › S

A Harmony of the Life of Jesus - The Sadducees: www.bible-history.com/jesus/jesusThe_Sadducees.htm

Sadducees - LoveToKnow 1911: www.1911encyclopedia.org/
Sadducees

The Sadducees | Bible.org - Worlds Largest Bible Study Site: bible.
org/seriespage/Sadducees

Bible Encyclopedia: Sadducees: bibleencyclopedia.com/sadducees.
htm

Sadducees (WebBible™ Encyclopedia) - ChristianAnswers.Net:
www.christiananswers.net/dictionary/sadducees.html

Ask the Pastor: Difference between Pharisees and Sadducees ...:
www.bethanybible.org/askpastor/pharsad.htm

The New Testament Jewish Sects: Pharisees, Sadducees, Essenes, Zealots:
www.bible.ca/d-jewish-sects-pharisees-sadducees-essenes-
zealots.htm

*Sadducees - Baker's Evangelical Dictionary of Biblical Theology
Online:*
www.biblestudytools.com/dictionaries/bakers.../sadducees.html
Sadducees – Conservapedia: www.conservapedia.com/
Sadducees

[PDF] The Sadducees: www.gracenotes.info/documents/
TOPICS_DOC/Sadducees.pdf

The Sadducees and Jesus - Question about Resurrection | Bible ...
bibleseo.com/luke/sadducees-jesus-question-resurrection/

Sadducees (Forerunner Commentary) :: Bible Tools:
www.bibletools.org/index.cfm/fuseaction/Topical.../Sadducees.
htm

[PDF] WHAT WERE THE SADDUCEES READING? AN ENQUIRY INTO THE LITERARY ...
www.tyndalehouse.com/.../TynBull_1994_45_2_08_Bolt_
SadduceesMk12. pdf

Essenes - Wikipedia, the free encyclopedia: en.wikipedia.org/wiki/
Essenes

Who were the Essenes?: www.essenespirit.com/who.html

CATHOLIC ENCYCLOPEDIA: Essenes:
www.newadvent.org › Catholic Encyclopedia › E

JewishEncyclopedia.com – ESSENES:
www.jewishencyclopedia.com/view.jsp?artid=478&letter...

Essenes, Essene Teachings and Essene Theology:
www.thenazareneway.com/

the essenes and the dead sea scrolls – PBS:
www.pbs.org/wgbh/pages/frontline/shows/.../essenes.html

The Essenes - The Essene New Testament - The Gospel of The Holy ...
reluctant-messenger.com/essene/index.html

Essene Nazarean Church of Mount Carmel: www.essene.com/

Introduction to the Ancient Essenes and the Modern Essene Church ...
www.essene.org/Ancient_Essenes.htm

Essenes: latter-rain.com/Israel/essenes.htm

Did the Essenes believe in some form of reincarnation?
www.spiritual-wholeness.org/faqs/reincgen/essrein.htm

Essenes - LoveToKnow 1911: www.1911encyclopedia.org/Essenes

Bible Study – Essenes: www.keyway.ca/htm2002/20020911. htm

The Essenes: www.realtime.net/~wdoud/topics/essenes.html

Josephus on the Essenes - Biblical Archaeology Review: www.bib-arch.org/e-features/josephus-essenes.asp

Essenes: Profile of the Essenes - Jewish Religious Group, Creators ... atheism.about.com › ... › Bible: New Testament People

[PDF] The Essenes: www.grandlodge.mb.ca/mrc_docs/Essenes.pdf

The Essenes - Answers.com: www.answers.com › ... › Literature & Language › Dictionary
Zealotry - Wikipedia, the free encyclopedia: en.wikipedia.org/ wiki/Zealotry

Zealots - LookLex Encyclopaedia: lexicorient.com/e.o/zealots. htm

JewishEncyclopedia.com – ZEALOTS: www.jewishencyclopedia.com/view.jsp?artid=49&letter=Z

Zealot (Judaism) -- Britannica Online Encyclopedia: www.britannica.com/EBchecked/topic/656131/Zealot

Zealots: latter-rain.com/ltrain/zeal.htm

The Zealots | Bible.org - Worlds Largest Bible Study Site: bible. org/seriespage/zealots

zealotry: Definition from Answers.com: www.answers.com › ... › Literature & Language › Dictionary

Zealots essays: www.megaessays.com/viewpaper/74464.html

Zealots – Definition: www.wordiq.com/definition/Zealots

[PDF] ON THE VALUE OF INTERTESTAMENTAL JEWISH LITERATURE FOR NEW ...
www.etsjets.org/files/JETS-PDFs/23/23-4/23-4-pp315-323_JETS.pdf

Cultural & Religious Background of Palestinian Judaism:
artfulword.org/word/hist/bckgrd2.htm

INTERTESTAMENTAL CULTURAL BACKGROUND HISTORY

Greek Culture: www.crystalinks.com/greekculture.html
Culture of Greece - Wikipedia, the free encyclopedia: en.wikipedia.org/wiki/Culture_of_Greece

Greece Culture: Information about the culture of Greece and the ...
www.greeka.com/greece-culture.htm

Greek Culture: www.buzzle.com/articles/greek-culture.html

Greece - Greek Language, Culture, Customs and Doing Business Etiquette
www.kwintessential.co.uk/.../greece-country-profile.html

Greek Care » Greek Culture and Tradition:
www.greekcare.org.au › Cultural Advice and Information
Culture of Greece - history, people, clothing, traditions, women ...
www.everyculture.com › Ge-It

Alexander Spreads Greek Culture - World History For Kids - By ...
www.kidspast.com/.../0075-alexander-spreads-greek-culture.php

Category:Greek culture - Wikipedia, the free encyclopedia
en.wikipedia.org/wiki/Category:Greek_culture

POLITICAL BACKGROUND HISTORY OF THE GOSPELS

Herod the Great - Wikipedia, the free encyclopedia
en.wikipedia.org/wiki/Herod_the_Great

King Herod the Great
www.livius.org/he-hg/herodians/herod_the_great01.html

Herod the Great Biography - life, family, death, wife, son ...
www.notablebiographies.com › He-Ho

History Crash Course #31: Herod the Great
www.aish.com/jl/h/48942446.html

Herod the Great - Flavius Josephus on How Herod the Great Became King
ancienthistory.about.com/od/.../a/herodthegreat.htm

CATHOLIC ENCYCLOPEDIA: Herod
www.newadvent.org › Catholic Encyclopedia › H

Herod the Great: Biography from Answers.com
www.answers.com › ... › Word Menu Categories

Herod the Great - King of the Jews
www.bible-history.com/herod_the_great/

Channel 4 - History - Herod the Great
www.channel4.com/history/.../herod.html - United Kingdom

Timeline results for "Herod the Great": www.helium.com

Herod the Great: crossfaithministry.org/herodthegreat.html

Herod (king of Judaea) -- Britannica Online Encyclopedia
www.britannica.com/EBchecked/topic/263437/Herod

Herod "the Great": www.tparents.org/Library/Religion/OTA/
OTA-Other/Herod.htm

The Lives of the Herod Family Intertwine with the Life of Jesus ...
www.sundayschoollessons.com/herod.htm

Herod the Great: www.vernonjohns.org/snuffy1186/herodgrt.html

Herod the Great (WebBible™ Encyclopedia) - ChristianAnswers.Net
www.christiananswers.net/dictionary/herodthegreat.html

Herod the Great: latter-rain.com/gospel/herodg.htm

King Herod the Great:
www.livius.org/he-hg/herodians/herod_the_great02.html

www.biblicalchronology.com/herod.htm

www.abu.nb.ca/courses/ntintro/intest/Hist6.htm

Herod the Great: Profile & Biography of Herod the Great, New ...
atheism.about.com › ... › Bible: New Testament People

Herod the Great and the Birth of Jesus: Gifts of the Magi, the ...
www.suite101.com/.../herod-the-great-and-the-birth-of-
jesus-a177107

Herod the Great - New World Encyclopedia
www.newworldencyclopedia.org/entry/Herod_the_Great

Daily Bible Study - Herod The Great: www.keyway.ca/htm2002/
herod.htm

Herod: virtualreligion.net/iho/herod_1.html

[PDF] Roman Government in Palestine From Herod the Great to the ...
web.mac.com/jimpapandrea/jimpapandrea.com/.../Palestine.pdf

Supplem ent 2: Herod the Great, King of the Jews: www. domainofman.com/book/sup2.html

What evidence is there for Herod the Great (the infanticide one ... uk.answers.yahoo.com › ... › Religion & Spirituality

Judean History: www.realtime.net/~wdoud/topics/judea.html

Herod the Great - Devotional Heart Message www.bible-history.com/herod_the_great/HEROD-heart-message.html

Herod the Great | Facebook: www.facebook.com/pages/Herod-the-Great/112442438774916

Herod the Great - The Second Temple: www.chabad.org/library/article_cdo/.../Herod-the-Great.htm

The Magi, the Massacre and Herod the Horrible « Alfred the Great ... atgsociety.com/2010/.../the-magi-the-massacre-and-herod-the-horrible/

How did Herod the Great die? - True Knowledge: www.trueknowledge.com/q/how_did_herod_the_great_die

Herod the Great - Everything on Herod the Great (information ... www.spiritus-temporis.com/herod-the-great/ - United States

[PDF] Herod: The Family of Herod the Great: www.swordofthespiritbibleministries.com/.../

Herod the Great: www.gracenotes.info/topics/herod.html

Herod the Great - Bible-Books-Maps.com: www.bible-books-maps.com/editorials/Herod-the-Great.asp

A General History of the Near East, Chapter 7: xenohistorian. faithweb.com/neareast/ne07.html

New Testament - Wikipedia, the free encyclopedia: en.wikipedia.org/wiki/New_Testament

The Whole Bible: New Testament History: www.maplenet. net/~trowbridge/NT_Hist.htm

Chronology of Early & New Testament Christianity: Christian ... atheism.about.com/library/FAQs/.../blchron_xian_nt.htm

New Testament Timeline: www.newtestamenthistorytimeline.com/

Timeline results for "New Testament History" www.deanburgonsociety.org

The New Testament - New Testament History: www.bible-history.com/resource/bi_new.htm

Is the Bible History or Myth: www.worldinvisible.com/apologet/ bible.htm

The New Testament: History's Verdict: www.bible.ca/ef/topical-the-new-testament-historys-verdict. htm

Category:New Testament history - Wikipedia, the free encyclopedia: en.wikipedia.org/wiki/Category:New_Testament_history

Jewish Groups in New Testament Times: catholic-resources.org/Bible/Jewish_Groups.htm

New Testament History Free Ebooks (pdf,doc,xls and etc.) ebookbrowse.com/search/new-testament-history

New Testament History Back Ground Free Essays 1 – 30
www.allfreeessays.com/topics/new-testament-history-background/0

Jewish Backgrounds of the New Testament www.spiritandtruth.org/.../review_of_jewish_backgrounds_of_the_nt.htm

CULTURAL BACKGROUND HISTORY OF THE GOSPELS

Cultural and historical background of Jesus - Wikipedia, the free ...
en.wikipedia.org/.../Cultural_and_historical_background_of_Jesus

Talk:Cultural and historical background of Jesus - Wikipedia, the ...
en.wikipedia.org/.../Talk%3ACultural_and_historical_background_of_Jesus

Cultural and historical background of Jesus
www.experiencefestival.com/cultural_and_historical_background_of_jesus

Cultural and Historical Background of Jesus - Secondary Sources
www.experiencefestival.com/cultural_and_historical_background_of_jesus _-_secondary_sources

Cultural and historical background of Jesus – Definition
www.wordiq.com/.../Cultural_and_historical_background_of_Jesus

Cultural and historical background of Jesus | Ask.com Encyclopedia
www.ask.com/wiki/Cultural_and_historical_background_of_Jesus

Cultural and historical background of Jesus - eNotes.com Reference
www.enotes.com/topic/Cultural_and_historical_background_of_Jesus

Cultural and historical background of Jesus - Religion-wiki
religion.wikia.com/.../Cultural_and_historical_background_of_Jesus

Jesus – Definition: www.wordiq.com/definition/Jesus

Cultural And Historical Background Of Jesus Information, Cultural ...
*reference.*findtarget.com/.../

Who is Jesus Christ ? » JESUS MISSION INTERNET EVANGELSM - GOD ..
www.peterpaul.tk/index.php?p=1_2_Who-is-Jesus-Christ

Judea and Samaria: en.academic.ru/dic.nsf/enwiki/226260

Judaea (Roman province) - Wikipedia, the free encyclopedia
en.wikipedia.org/wiki/Judaea_(Roman_province)